Readings in Literary Criticism 21

CRITICS ON MARK TWAIN

Readings in Literary Criticism

CRITICS ON
MARK TWAIN

Readings in Literary Criticism
Edited by David B. Kesterson

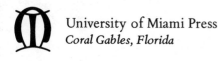
University of Miami Press
Coral Gables, Florida

Library of Congress Cataloging in Publication Data

Kesterson, David B   1938-   comp.
    Critics on Mark Twain.

    (Readings in literary criticism, 21)
    Bibliography: p.
    1. Clemens, Samuel Langhorne, 1835-1910.
I. Title.
PS1338.K4   818' .4'09   73-77553
ISBN 0-87024-251-2

CONTENTS

6 CONTENTS

ACKNOWLEDGMENTS

Frank Baldanza: from *Mark Twain: An Introduction and Interpretation.* Copyright 1961 by Barnes & Noble, Inc. Reprinted by permission of the publisher.

Gladys C. Bellamy: from *Mark Twain As a Literary Artist* by Gladys Carmen Bellamy. Copyright 1950 by the University of Oklahoma Press. Reprinted by permission of the publisher.

Minnie N. Brashear: from *Mark Twain: Son of Missouri.* Copyright 1934 by the University of North Carolina Press. Reprinted by permission of the publisher.

Van Wyck Brooks: from *The Ordeal of Mark Twain* by Van Wyck Brooks. Copyright 1920 by E. P. Dutton & Co., Inc. Renewal, 1948, by Van Wyck Brooks. Published by E. P. Dutton & Co., Inc. and used with their permission.

Henry S. Canby: from *Turn West, Turn East.* Copyright 1951 by Henry Seidel Canby. Reprinted by permission of the publisher, Houghton Mifflin Company.

Pascal Covici, Jr.: from *Mark Twain's Humor.* Copyright 1962 by Southern Methodist University Press. Reprinted by permission of the publisher.

Alexander Cowie: from *The Rise of the American Novel.* Copyright 1948 by American Book Company. Reprinted by permission of the publisher.

Bernard De Voto: from *Mark Twain's America.* Copyright renewed 1960 by Avis M. De Voto (originally 1932 by Bernard De Voto). Reprinted by permission of the publisher, Houghton Mifflin Company.

William B. Dillingham: from *Mark Twain Journal,* 12 (Spring 1964), 6-8. Reprinted by permission of the publisher.

T. S. Eliot: from "Introduction" to *Huckleberry Finn.* Reprinted by permission of Mrs. Valerie Eliot.

Allison Ensor: from *Mark Twain & the Bible.* Copyright 1969 by The University Press of Kentucky. Reprinted by permission of the publisher.

Judith Fetterley: from *Studies in the Novel,* 3 (Fall 1971), 293-304. Copyright 1971 by North Texas State University. Reprinted by permission of the publisher.

Robert M. Gay: from *Atlantic Monthly,* 165 (Dec. 1940), 724-26. Copyright © 1940, R 1948, by The Atlantic Monthly Company, Boston, Mass. Reprinted with permission.

Maxwell Geismar: from *Mark Twain: An American Prophet.* Copyright 1970 by Maxwell Geismar. Reprinted by permission of the publisher, Houghton Mifflin Company.

Allen Guttmann: from *The New England Quarterly,* 33 (June 1960), 232-37. Copyright 1960 by *The New England Quarterly.* Reprinted by permission of the author and the publisher.

F. R. Leavis: Copyright © 1955 by F. R. Leavis. Reprinted from *Anna Karenina and Other Essays,* by permission of the author, Pantheon Books / a Division of Random House, Inc., and Chatto and Windus Ltd.

Marion Montgomery: from *The Mississippi Quarterly,* 11 (1958), 79-82. Copyright 1958 by *The Mississippi Quarterly.* Reprinted by permission of the publisher.

Charles Neider: Reprinted by permission of the publisher, Horizon Press, New York, from *Mark Twain* by Charles Neider, copyright 1967.

V. L. Parrington: from *The Beginnings of Critical Realism in America.* Copyright 1930 by Harcourt, Brace & Co., Inc. Reprinted by permission of the publishers, Harcourt Brace Jovanovich, Inc.

Bliss Perry: from "The American Spirit in Literature" by Bliss Perry, Vol. 34 in *The Chronicles of America.* Sole distributor United States Publishers Association, Inc.

A. H. Quinn: from *American Fiction.* Copyright 1936 by D. Appleton-Century Co. Reprinted by permission of Appleton-Century-Crofts.

Arthur L. Scott: from *Western Humanities Review*, 7 (Summer 1953), 215-23. Copyright 1953 by the University of Utah. Reprinted by permission of the author and *Western Humanities Review.*

Martin S. Schockley: from *The South-Central Bulletin,* 20 (Winter 1960), 3-10. Reprinted by permission of the author and the publisher.

Henry Nash Smith: Reprinted by permission of the publishers from pp. 113-14 and 118-22 of Henry Nash Smith, *Mark Twain: The Development of a Writer,* Cambridge, Mass.: The Belknap Press of Harvard University Press, Copyright 1962, by the President and Fellows of Harvard College.

Robert E. Spiller: Reprinted by permission of Macmillan Publishing Co., Inc. from *The Cycle of American Literature*, by Robert E. Spiller. Copyright 1955, 1956 by The Macmillan Company.

Floyd Stovall: from *American Idealism*, by Floyd Stovall. Copyright 1943 by The University of Oklahoma Press. Reprinted by permission of the publisher.

Carl Van Doren: Reprinted with permission of Macmillan Publishing Co., Inc. from *The American Novel, 1789-1939* (Revised) by Carl Van Doren. Copyright 1921, 1940 by The Macmillan Company: renewed 1949 by Carl Van Doren, and 1968 by Anne Van Doren Ross, Barbara Van Doren Klaw, and Margaret Van Doren Bevans.

Mark Van Doren: from *The Nation,* 141 (October 23, 1935), 473. Copyright by *The Nation.* Reprinted by permission of the publisher.

Edward Wagenknecht: from *Cavalcade of the American Novel*, by Edward Wagenknecht. Copyright 1952 by Holt, Rinehart and Winston, Inc. Reprinted by permission of Holt, Rinehart and Winston, Inc.

Edward Wagenknecht: from *Mark Twain: The Man and His Work*, by Edward Wagenknecht. Revised edition copyright 1961 by the University of Oklahoma Press. Reprinted by permission of the publisher.

Larzer Ziff: from *The American 1890s: Life and Times of a Lost Generation,* by Larzer Ziff. Copyright © 1966 by Larzer Ziff. Reprinted by permission of The Viking Press, Inc.

INTRODUCTION

THE COMIC genius of Mark Twain was recognized throughout America with the publication of his "Jumping Frog" story, his early success on the lecture platform, and the series of humorous travel letters he wrote from Europe and the Holy Land to American newspapers. All these events took place in the late 1860s. It was as this comic genius, a literary funny man, that the remaining thirty years of nineteenth-century America mainly received and understood Twain. He was, in his writings, more prolific and ambitious than other literary comedians such as Artemus Ward and Josh Billings; but he was definitely the comedian, the court jester who delighted lyceum audiences with his droll wit and charmed readers with his humorous tales and clever journalism. Only a few critics, such as Brander Matthews and Twain's close friend William Dean Howells, saw beneath the comic veneer to the deeper, more serious artist that lay beneath the surface. That their view would dominate twentieth-century criticism would have been as surprising to Twain's contemporaries as his being awarded the Litt.D. degree by Oxford University in 1907, an act revealing British acceptance of Twain as a major literary figure.

Criticism awakened early in the twentieth century to the serious artist behind the comedian, and by the half-century mark hundreds of books and articles had attested to the many facets of Twain's talent: Twain and southwestern humor, Twain and the art of the novel, Twain and platform lecturing, Twain and the art of the short story, Twain and the picaresque tradition, Twain and social criticism, etc. Of all these studies, four works before 1950 stand out above others as formative and essential to what developed later in Twain biography and criticism. The four are Albert Bigelow Paine's _Mark Twain: A Biography_ (1912), Van Wyck Brooks' _The Ordeal of Mark Twain_ (1920), Bernard De Voto's _Mark Twain's America_ (1932), and DeLancey Ferguson's _Mark Twain: Man and Legend_ (1943). Paine's monumental, if somewhat sentimental, biography brought the facts of Twain's long, action-filled life into focus and provided invaluable information for others to work with. Brooks' volume began the critical debate over whether Twain was a thwarted artist, trapped by the philistinism of the Victorian age, his geographical region, and his boyhood family—a view De Voto counterattacked in _Mark Twain's America_. De Voto rose to the defense of

Twain's frontier background and showed how it led to, rather than detracted from, the growth of the artist. Coming several years after the famous Brooks-De Voto feud had cooled, Ferguson's biography offered a more balanced view of Twain; it is still considered a first-rate biography and a highly useful source.

Since mid-century, a veritable Twainian explosion has rocked the scholarly world, producing outstanding biographies and critical books and articles by such names as Dixon Wecter, Henry Nash Smith, Gladys Bellamy, Henry S. Canby, Edward Wagenknecht, Kenneth Andrews, Frank Baldanza, James Cox, and Justin Kaplan. The Twain explosion has also resulted in the exciting publishing ventures of *The Mark Twain Papers* (University of California, Berkeley) and the new California-Iowa edition of Twain's works. A spate of recent studies, moreover, takes new looks at the Twain books so long ignored critically, such as *Life on the Mississippi, Pudd'nhead Wilson,* and especially *Tom Sawyer.* In all aspects, then, this is definitely Twain's day.

It is my intention in this book to capture the history of the lively and variable progression of Twain criticism from his own times to the present. Presented here are a hundred years of reactions to a man and writer who above all remains an enigma in world literature. Here are the favorable and unfavorable, the limited and the broad, the astute and a bit of the obtuse. Through all, however, there is a certain implied direction, one moving to the ultimate conclusion that Twain, the nineteenth century's consummate comedian, is without doubt now recognized as the master of letters with as many sides to his nature and art as there are approaches in his dynamic works themselves.

North Texas State University, 1973   DAVID B. KESTERSON

TABLE OF IMPORTANT DATES

1835	Samuel Langhorne Clemens born in Florida, Missouri, November 30.
1839	Clemens family moved to Hannibal, Missouri.
1847	John Marshall Clemens died in March. Samuel Clemens worked as printer following father's death.
1853-54	Clemens traveled east of the Mississippi, working as journalist and printer.
1855-56	Worked as a printer for brother Orion in Keokuk, Iowa.
1857	Arrived in New Orleans intending to go to South America, but met pilot Horace Bixby, who consented to teach Clemens to pilot a steamboat.
1858	Learned the Mississippi River and became a pilot.
1861	Civil War closed the river to steamboating. Twain saw brief military service, then took twenty-one-day journey by stagecoach to Carson City, Nevada, in late July and early August.
1862	In August joined staff of *Virginia City Territorial Enterprise,* remaining there until May 1864.
1863	February 2 first signed name "Mark Twain" in a dispatch to the *Enterprise* from Carson City. In December met Artemus Ward in Virginia City.
1864	Became involved in dispute with another editor, leading to a proposed duel (violating Nevada law) that caused Twain to leave for San Francisco.
1865	Published "Jim Smiley and His Jumping Frog" in the New York *Saturday Press.*
1866	Spent four months in Sandwich Islands writing series of travel letters for the Sacramento *Union.* In October began career of platform lecturing in San Francisco. Popularity led to tour of California and Nevada and brought wide-reaching fame.
1867	*The Celebrated Jumping Frog of Calaveras County, and Other Sketches* published in New York. In June sailed for Holy Land excursion as correspondent for the San Francisco *Alto California.*
1869	*The Innocents Abroad* published.

1869-70	Lectured with James Redpath's Boston Lyceum Bureau.
1870	Married Olivia Langdon on February 2. Langdon Clemens prematurely born November 7 in Buffalo.
1871	Moved to Hartford, Connecticut, renting a house at Nook Farm.
1872	*Roughing It* published in February. Olivia Susan Clemens born on March 19. Langdon Clemens died June 2.
1873	*The Gilded Age* published in collaboration with Charles Dudley Warner.
1874	Clara Clemens born in June.
1876	*The Adventures of Tom Sawyer* published in December.
1877	Produced a play *Ah Sin* in collaboration with Bret Harte. On December 17 made notorious Whittier birthday speech in Boston.
1878-79	Lived in Germany and Italy.
1880	*A Tramp Abroad* published. Jean Clemens born July 26.
1882	*The Prince and the Pauper* published. In April-May returned to the Mississippi River for trip to New Orleans and a reunion with Horace Bixby.
1883	*Life on the Mississippi* published.
1884	Lecture tours with George Washington Cable in November and December.
1885	Published *Adventures of Huckleberry Finn* in January, followed by General Grant's *Memoirs* in the fall.
1889	Published *A Connecticut Yankee in King Arthur's Court.*
1890	Worked on the Paige typesetting machine.
1892	Published *The American Claimant.*
1894	*Tom Sawyer Abroad* published in spring, followed in November by *Pudd'nhead Wilson.*
1896	Susy, Twain's favorite child, died August 18. In November appeared *Tom Sawyer Abroad, Tom Sawyer, Detective, and Other Stories.*
1897	*Following the Equator* published in November.
1900	Published *The Man that Corrupted Hadleyburg and Other Stories and Essays.*
1904	Olivia Langdon Clemens died June 5.
1907	Twain honored with a Litt.D. degree from Oxford University.
1909	Jean Clemens died.
1910	Twain died April 21 and was buried at Elmira, New York.
1916	*The Mysterious Stranger* published.
1917	*What Is Man? and Other Essays* appeared.

Critics on Mark Twain: 1882-1940

WILLIAM DEAN HOWELLS: 1882, 1901, 1910

Assessments by a Friend

I SUPPOSE that Mark Twain transcends all other American humorists in the universal qualities. He deals very little with the pathetic, which he nevertheless knows very well how to manage, as he has shown, notably in the true story of the old slave-mother; but there is a poetic lift in his work, even when he permits you to recognize it only as something satirized. There is always the touch of nature, the presence of a sincere and frank manliness in what he says, the companionship of a spirit which is at once delightfully open and deliciously shrewd. Elsewhere I have tried to persuade the reader that his humor is at its best the foamy break of the strong tide of earnestness in him. But it would be limiting him unjustly to describe him as a satirist; and it is hardly practicable to establish him in people's minds as a moralist; he has made them laugh too long; they will not believe him serious; they think some joke is always intended. This is the penalty, as Dr. Holmes has pointed out, of making one's first success as a humorist.

From "Mark Twain," *The Century Magazine,* 24 (September 1882), 782.

One of the characteristics I observe in him is his single-minded use of words, which he employs as Grant did to express the plain, straight meaning their common acceptance has given them with no regard to their structural significance or their philological implications. He writes English as if it were a primitive and not a derivative language, without Gothic or Latin or Greek behind it, or German and French beside it. The result is the English in which the most vital works of English literature are cast, rather than the English of Milton, and Thackeray, and Mr. Henry James. I do not say that the English of the authors last named is less than vital, but only that it is not the most vital. It is scholarly and conscious; it knows who its grandfather was; it has the refinement and subtlety of an old patriciate. You will not have with it the widest suggestion, the largest human feeling, or perhaps the loftiest reach of imagination, but you will have the keen joy that exquisite artistry in words can alone impart, and that you will not have in Mark Twain. What you will have in him is a style which is as personal, as biographical as the style of any one who has written, and expresses a civilization whose courage of the chances, the preferences, the duties, is not the measure of its essential modesty. It has a thing to say, and it says it in the word that may be the first, or second, or third choice, but will not be the instrument of the most fastidious ear, the most delicate and exacting sense, though it will be the word that surely and strongly conveys intention from the author's mind to the reader's. It is the Abraham Lincolnian word, not the Charles Sumnerian; it is American, Western.

From "Mark Twain: An Inquiry," *North American Review,* 172 (February 1901), 309.

He had always a relish for personal effect, which expressed itself in the white suit of complete serge which he wore in his last years, and in the Oxford gown which he put on for every possible occasion, and said he would like to wear all the time. That was not vanity in him, but a keen feeling for costume which the severity of our modern tailoring forbids men, though it flatters women to every excess in it; yet he also enjoyed the shock, the offence, the pang which it gave the sensibilities of others. Then there were times he played these pranks for pure fun, and for the pleasure of the witness. Once I remember seeing him come into his drawing-room at Hartford in a pair of white cowskin slippers, with the hair out, and do a crippled colored uncle to the joy of all beholders. Or, I must not say all, for I remember also the dismay of Mrs. Clemens, and her low, despairing cry of, "Oh, Youth!" That was her name for him among their friends, and it fitted him as no other would, though I fancied with her it was a shrinking from his baptismal Samuel, or the vernacular Sam of his earlier companionships. He was a youth to the end of his days, the heart of a boy with the head of a sage; the heart of a good boy, or a bad boy, but always a wilful boy, and wilfulest to show himself out at every time for just the boy he was.

From *My Mark Twain: Reminiscences and Criticism* (New York: Harper & Brothers, 1910), pp. 4-5.

JOHN NICHOL: 1882

An American Philistine

IT IS PROBABLE that, to the lower class of British Philistines, American prose is, at this day, represented not so much by Irving, Emerson, or Hawthorne, as by "Mark Twain," who has done perhaps more than any other living writer to lower the literary tone of English speaking people. The most conspicuous intellectual trait of Mr. Clemens seems to me an almost preternatural shrewdness, thinly veiled under an assumption of simplicity. He knows perfectly what he is about, and is able to turn every incident or circumstance to his advantage. He prefixes a recent paper, "The Idle Excursion," with the remark, "All the journeyings I have done had been purely in the way of business. The pleasant May weather suggested a novelty, a trip for pure recreation, the bread and butter element left out:" but he writes seventy pages about the trip; and so provides for the element ostentatiously neglected. Of the alarming tribe of recent American cynics he is the most genuine. He hates humbug and cant, and nothing delights him more than to run a tilt at copy-book texts. It goes without saying that his "bad little boy" will prosper, and his "good little boy" come to grief; or that he will give an absurd turn to the story of Washington and the cherry-tree. Romance and sentiment, in either continent, fare equally at his hands: "Old masters" at Milan, Florence, and Rome are served in the same manner as the journalists in Tennessee; he writes his text to the sketch of a weazened hag perched on the summit of the Loreley Rock; makes a grimace at the Pyramids; puts his finger to his nose among the Alps; and, as it were, turning the statues in the Louvre, the Uffizi, and the Vatican, upside down, inspects their legs. But, if his scepticism is intense, his morality is truculent: he visits the tomb of Abelard, and pronounces a blessing on his semi-assassins; and his blushes are blent with curses over Regent Street.

Mark Twain's attraction is due in great measure to his freshness: he is not an imitator; he does not rely on books—though his writings evince a more than average culture: he is a parodist of his own experience, to which he holds up a mirror, like one of the round balls in German gardens.

> "Life's a jest, and all things show it;
> I thought so once, and now I know it,"

is the refrain of his philosophy. His satire, unlike that of "Billings," is conveyed not so much in dogmatic sentences as in often dramatic narrative.

From "Mark Twain," *American Literature: An Historical Sketch, 1620-1880* (Edinburgh: Adam & Charles Black, 1882), pp. 426-27.

CONCORD PUBLIC LIBRARY: 1885

The Banning of *Huckleberry Finn*

THE CONCORD (Mass.) Public Library committee has decided to exclude Mark Twain's latest book from the library. One member of the committee says that, while he does not wish to call it immoral, he thinks it contains but little humor, and that of a very coarse type. He regards it as the veriest trash. The librarian and the other members of the committee entertain similar views, characterizing it as rough, coarse and inelegant, dealing with a series of experiences not elevating, the whole book being more suited to the slums than to intelligent, respectable people.

From the Boston *Transcript,* March 17, 1885.

JOEL CHANDLER HARRIS: 1885

Perennial Youth in Twain

AND YET I am glad that he is fifty years old. He has earned the right
to grow old and mellow. He has put his youth in his books, and there it
is perennial. His last book is better than his first, and there his youth is
renewed and revived. I know that some of the professional critics will
not agree with me, but there is not in our fictive literature a more
wholesome book than 'Huckleberry Finn.' It is history, it is romance, it
is life. Here we behold human character stripped of all tiresome details;
we see people growing and living; we laugh at their humor, share their
griefs; and, in the midst of it all, behold we are taught the lesson of
honesty, justice and mercy.

From *The Critic,* n.s., 4 (November 28, 1885), 253.

OLIVER WENDELL HOLMES: 1885

To Mark Twain (on His Fiftieth Birthday)

Ah Clemens, when I saw thee last,—
  We both of us were younger,—
How fondly mumbling o'er the past
  Is Memory's toothless hunger!

So fifty years have fled, they say,
  Since first you took to drinking,—
I mean in Nature's milky way,—
  Of course no ill I'm thinking.

But while on life's uneven road
  Your track you've been pursuing,
What fountains from your wit have flowed—
  What drinks you have been brewing!

I know whence all your magic came,—
  Your secret I've discovered,—
The source that fed your inward flame—
  The dreams that round you hovered:

Before you learned to bite or munch
  Still kicking in your cradle,
The Muses mixed a bowl of punch
  And Hebe seized the ladle.

Dear babe, whose fiftieth year to-day
  Your ripe half-century rounded,
Your books the precious draught betray
  The laughing Nine compounded.

So mixed the sweet, the sharp, the strong,
  Each finds its faults amended,
The virtues that to each belong
  In happier union blended.

And what the flavor can surpass
Of sugar, spirit, lemons?
So while one health fills every glass
Mark Twain for Baby Clemens!

From *The Critic,* n.s., 4 (November 28, 1885), 253.

ANDREW LANG: 1891

Tempered Praise

IF YOU praise him among persons of Culture, they cannot believe that you are serious. They call him a Barbarian. They won't hear of him, they hurry from the subject; they pass by on the other side of the way. Now I do not mean to assert that Mark Twain is 'an impeccable artist,' but he is just as far from being a mere coarse buffoon. Like other people, he has his limitations. Even Mr. Gladstone, for instance, does not shine as a Biblical critic, nor Mark Twain as a critic of Italian art nor as a guide to the Holy Land. I have abstained from reading his work on an American at the Court of King Arthur, because here Mark Twain is not, and cannot be, at the proper point of view. He has not the knowledge which would enable him to be a sound critic of the ideal of the Middle Ages. An Arthurian Knight in New York or in Washington would find as much to blame, and justly, as a Yankee at Camelot. Let it be admitted that Mark Twain often and often sins against good taste, that some of his waggeries are mechanical, that his books are full of passages which were only good enough for the corner of a newspaper.

From "Mr. Lang on the Art of Mark Twain," *The Critic*, n.s., 16 (July 25, 1891), 45-46.

REV. JOSEPH H. TWICHELL: 1896

What Price Humor?

SOME OF those who know him best have strongly felt that he was capable of literary production in other lines that those in which he has wrought, which, if less popular, would more amply have exhibited the higher range of his powers as a cultivated thinking man. Had he not, indeed, begun with "managing" (to quote the recent expression of a New Zealand journal) "to tickle the midriff of the English-speaking races," and so made it an inexorable and fated thing, as it were, by the compulsory force of public expectation, that his permanent principal *rôle* should be that of humorist, there is no telling what he might have done. The consideration, however, of what has thus been possibly missed will scarcely produce widespread grief.

From "Mark Twain," *Harper's Magazine,* 92 (May 1896), 822.

BRANDER MATTHEWS: 1907, 1920

Twain's Universal Appeal and His Use of Language

IN LIKE manner the American author who has chosen to call himself Mark Twain has attained to an immense popularity because the qualities he possesses in a high degree appeal to so many and so widely varied publics,—first of all, no doubt, to the public that revels in hearty and robust fun, but also to the public which is glad to be swept along by the full current of adventure, which is sincerely touched by manly pathos, which is satisfied by vigorous and exact portrayal of character, which respects shrewdness and wisdom and sanity and which appreciates a healthy hatred of pretense and affectation and sham. Perhaps no one book of Mark Twain's—with the possible exception of 'Huckleberry Finn'—is equally a favorite with all his readers; and perhaps some of his best characteristics are absent from his earlier books or but doubtfully latent in them. Mark Twain is many-sided; and he has ripened in knowledge and in power since he first attracted attention as a wild Western funny man. As he has grown older he has reflected more; he has both broadened and deepened. The writer of "comic copy" for a mining-camp newspaper has developed into a liberal humorist, handling life seriously and making his readers think as he makes them laugh, until to-day Mark Twain has perhaps the largest audience of any author now using the English language.

From *Inquiries and Opinions* (New York: Charles Scribner's Sons, 1907), pp. 140-41.

He selected for his composition the best in spoken use. He profited by one of the advantages of writing as we speak, if only we are in the habit of speaking with due respect for the nobility of our tongue, that he did not cumber his pages with dead and gone words. Like every growing language, English has a host of words which have fallen into innocuous desuetude and are no longer understanded [sic] of the people. They may run off the pen of the pedantic, but they never fall from the lips of Mark Twain. He was a man of his own time, with no hankering after the archaic. His language is the living speech of those who have English for their mother-tongue, however scattered they may be on all the shores of all the seven seas. . . .

It must be noted also that Mark refrained from the employment of the newest words, the linguistic novelties which are on probation, as it were, which may in time win acceptance, but which for the moment are only colloquialisms, uncertain of their ultimate admission into the vocabulary as desirable citizens.

From "Mark Twain and the Art of Writing," *Harper's Magazine,* 14 (October 1920), 637.

GEORGE ADE: 1910

"The Best of Our Emissaries"

FURTHERMORE is it not possible that much of the tremendous liking for Mark Twain grew out of his success in establishing our credit abroad? Any American who can invade Europe and command respectful attention is entitled to triumphal arches when he arrives home. Our dread and fear of foreign criticism are still most acute. . . . But Mark Twain was probably the best of our emissaries. He never waved the starry banner and at the same time he never went around begging forgiveness. He knew the faults of his home people, and he understood intimately and with a family knowledge all of their good qualities and groping intentions and half-formed plans for big things in the future; but apparently he did not think it necessary to justify all of his private beliefs to men who lived five thousand miles away from Hannibal, Missouri. He had been in all parts of the world and had made a calm and unbiased estimate of the relative values of men and institutions. Probably he came to know that all had been cut from one piece and then trimmed variously. He carried with him the same placid habits of life that sufficed him in Connecticut, and because he was what he pretended to be, the hypercritical foreigners doted upon him and the Americans at home, glad to flatter themselves, said, "Why, certainly, he's one of us."

From "Mark Twain as Our Emissary," *The Century Magazine,* 81 (December 1910), 205-6.

ALBERT BIGELOW PAINE: 1912

Twain as Comic Lecturer

HIS USUAL formula was to present himself as the chairman of the committee, introducing the lecturer of the evening; then, with what was in effect a complete change of personality, to begin his lecture. It was always startling and amusing, always a success; but the papers finally printed his formula, which took the freshness out of it, so that he had to invent others. Sometimes he got up with the frank statement that he was introducing himself because he had never met any one who could pay a proper tribute to his talents; but the newspapers printed that too, and he often rose and began with no introduction at all.

Whatever his method of beginning, Mark Twain's procedure probably was the purest exemplification of the platform entertainer's art which this country has ever seen. It was the art that makes you forget the artisanship, the art that made each hearer forget that he was not being personally entertained by a new and marvelous friend, who had traveled a long way for his particular benefit. One listener has written that he sat "simmering with laughter" through what he supposed was the continuation of the introduction, waiting for the traditional lecture to begin, when presently the lecturer, with a bow, disappeared, and it was over. The listener looked at his watch; he had been there more than an hour. He thought it could be no more than ten minutes, at most. Many have tried to set down something of the effect his art produced on them, but one may not clearly convey the story of a vanished presence and a silent voice.

From *Mark Twain: A Biography* (New York: Harper & Brothers, 1912), Vol. 2, p. 447.

F. L. PATTEE: 1915

America's First Native Writer

WITH MARK TWAIN, American literature became for the first time really national. He was the first man of letters of any distinction to be born west of the Mississippi. He spent his boyhood and young manhood near the heart of the continent, along the great river during the vital era when it was the boundary line between known and unknown America, and when it resounded from end to end with the shouts and the confusion of the first great migration from the East; he lived for six thrilling years in the camps and the boom towns and the excited cities of Nevada and California; and then, at thirty-one, a raw product of the raw West, he turned his face to the Atlantic Coast, married a rare soul from one of the refined families of New York State, and settled down to a literary career in New England, with books and culture and trips abroad, until in his old age Oxford University could confer upon him— "Tom Sawyer," whose schooling in the ragged river town had ended before he was twelve—the degree that had come to America only as borne by two or three of the Brahmins of New England. Only America, and America at a certain period, could produce a paradox like that.

Mark Twain interpreted the West from the standpoint of a native. The group of humorists who had first brought to the East the Western spirit and the new laughter had all of them been reared in the older sections. John Phoenix and Artemus Ward and Josh Billings were born in New England, and Nasby and many of the others were natives of New York State. All of them in late boyhood had gone West as to a wonderland and had breathed the new atmosphere as something strange and exhilarating, but Mark Twain was native born. He was himself a part of the West; he removed from it so as to see it in true perspective, and so became its best interpreter. Hawthorne had once expressed a wish to see some part of America "where the damned shadow of Europe has never fallen." Mark Twain spent his life until he was thirty in such unshadowed places. When he wrote he wrote without a thought of other writings; it was as if the West itself was dictating its autobiography.

From *A History of American Literature Since 1870* (New York: Century, 1915), pp. 45-46.

BLISS PERRY: 1918

Romancer Transcends Humorist

IT IS CLEAR that Mark Twain the writer of romance is gaining upon Mark Twain the humorist. The inexhaustible American appetite for frontier types of humor seizes upon each new variety, crunches it with huge satisfaction, and then tosses it away. John Phoenix, Josh Billings, Jack Downing, Bill Arp, Petroleum V. Nasby, Artemus Ward, Bill Nye—these are already obsolescent names. If Clemens lacked something of Artemus Ward's whimsical delicacy and of Josh Billings's tested human wisdom, he surpassed all of his competitors in a certain rude, healthy masculinity, the humor of river and mining-camp and printing-office, where men speak without censorship. His country-men liked exaggeration, and he exaggerated; they liked irreverence, and he had turned iconoclast in *Innocents Abroad*. As a professional humorist, he has paid the obligatory tax for his extravagance, over-emphasis, and undisciplined taste, but such faults are swiftly forgotten when one turns to Huckleberry Finn and the negro Jim and Pudd'nhead Wilson, when one feels Mark Twain's power in sheer description and episode, his magic in evoking landscape and atmosphere, his blazing scorn at injustice and cruelty, his contempt for quacks.

From *The American Spirit in Literature* (New Haven: Yale Univ. Press, 1918), pp. 239-40.

VAN WYCK BROOKS: 1920

"Circumstances . . . Overwhelmingly Unfavorable"

IN ALL his environment, then, we see, there was nothing to assist in the transformation of an unconscious artistic instinct, however urgent, into a conscious artistic purpose. "Dahomey," wrote Mark Twain once, "could not find an Edison out; in Dahomey an Edison could not find himself out. Broadly speaking, genius is not born with sight but blind; and it is not itself that opens its eyes, but the subtle influences of a myriad of stimulating exterior circumstances." He was reciting his own story in those words. But the circumstances that surrounded Mark Twain were not merely passively unfavorable to his own self-discovery; they were actively, overwhelmingly unfavorable. He was in his mother's leading-strings, and in his mother's eyes any sort of personal self-assertion in choices, preferences, impulses was, literally, sinful. Thus the whole weight of the Calvinistic tradition was concentrated against him at his most vulnerable point. His mother, whom he could not gainsay, was unconsciously but inflexibly set against his genius; and destiny, which always fights on the side of the heaviest artillery, delivered, in his twelfth year, a stroke that sealed her victory.

Mark Twain's father died.

From *The Ordeal of Mark Twain* (New York: Dutton, 1920), p. 39.

LUCY L. HAZARD: 1927

Satirist of the "Gilded Age"

MARK TWAIN, while profiting from the Gilded Age, wrote of it with a fierce undercurrent of savage criticism. The extent to which this criticism was suppressed or modified, the reasons for its suppression and modification, and the effect of this censorship of the genius of Mark Twain, have been brilliantly suggested by Van Wyck Brooks in *The Ordeal of Mark Twain.* Like most theses, this book suffers from its attempt to prove too much; intrigued by a Freudian curiosity concerning Mark Twain's wife and mother, Mr. Brooks is diverted from a consideration of Mark Twain's social purposes to an investigation of his personal complexes. The newest of critical methods results in the old *Cherchez la femme:* the women in the case are found responsible for the alleged miscarriage of Mark Twain's genius. Absorbed in the decanonization of "Livy," Mr. Brooks loses sight of the larger social group whose standards, motives, and activities made up the *Zeitgeist* of the sensational seventies; he underestimates the extent to which Mark Twain was himself a product of the Gilded Age, like Hawthorne impotently critical of the forces which had entered into the very fiber of his being. . . . The fatal cleavage which Mr. Brooks has traced in his nature represents not so much superimposed inhibitions of Howells, of *The Atlantic Monthly,* of Mrs. Clemens, as a divided self which, on the one hand, admires the gentility, the ease, the power, which are the rewards of success, and on the other, has a tenderness for the pathetic fools of fortune, a fierce contempt for the hypocrisy and greed and cruelty underlying the social conspiracy which assures the success of the successful. Hence even in his gayest writings about the Gilded Age there is a note of satire.

From *The Frontier in American Literature* (New York: Crowell, 1927), pp. 220-23.

V. L. PARRINGTON: 1930

A "Significant American Document"

YET WITH all his shortcomings—because of them indeed—Mark Twain is an immensely significant American document. He is a mirror reflecting the muddy cross-currents of American life as the frontier spirit washed in, submerging the old aristocratic landmarks. To know Mark Twain is to know the strange and puzzling contradictions of the Gilded Age. With unconscious fidelity he reveals its crudity, its want of knowledge, discipline, historical perspective; its intellectual incapacity to deal with the complexities of a world passing through the twin revolutions of industrialism and science. And he reflects with equal fidelity certain other qualities that go far to redeem the meanness: a great creative power; an eager idealism, somewhat vague but still fine; a generous sympathy; a manly independence that strove to think honestly; a passionate hatred of wrong and injustice and an honest democratic respect for men as men. A significant if not an unsoiled or heroic document!

From *The Beginnings of Critical Realism in America, 1860-1900* (New York: Harcourt, Brace, 1930), p. 88.

BERNARD DE VOTO: 1932

Answer to Van Wyck Brooks

THE INITIAL undertaking of Mr. Brooks's psycho-analysis is to discover why Mark Twain, a man of genius, fame, wealth, and happy social relations was a pessimist. The presence of cynical and bitter passages in his works and letters required explanation, although no explanation of his laughter and good nature was required. The need grew out of a discomfort traditional to criticism in America: the literature of disillusionment has always had to be explained as something other than the sense of reality. At the beginning of his search, Mr. Brooks assumes that this pessimism was the product of an unconscious conflict, a sense of guilt, a symptom that Mark Twain was a divided soul. Having made this assumption, he then uses it to prove itself.

The basic conflict is derived by assumption. Mark Twain was born, Mr. Brooks says, to be a literary artist. Here the eidolon appears. An "artist", to Mr. Brooks, is a person who rebels against authority. Literature is "a great impersonal social instrument." The root of Mr. Brooks's theory is plain: it is a moralist's dislike of all art that does not demand political or economic reform. Popular psycho-analysis derives the careers of revolutionists from juvenile revolt against the authority of parents: literary theory substitutes Shelley for Samuel Adams but retains the mechanism intact.

For evidence of Mark Twain's predestined greatness as a "pure" artist Mr. Brooks offers the admissions of Mr. Paine that up to the age of twelve Mark was a mischievous child who played pranks, sometimes disobeyed his parents, and had an aversion to school. (It must be borne in mind that a great part of this psycho-analysis is applied to Mr. Paine's book, not to Mark Twain.) No further evidence is offered: none exists. Mark Twain was clearly designed to be an artist, in rebellion against the Philistinism of America, because he played pirate and absented himself from school. These diversions were "the first stirrings of the normal aesthetic sense, the first stirrings of individuality."

From *Mark Twain's America* (Boston: Little, Brown, 1932), pp. 229-30.

MINNIE N. BRASHEAR: 1934

A Challenge to Critics

NO AMERICAN writer has offered a more insistent challenge to critics than Mark Twain. The early popularity of his humorous lectures was much extended by the publication under his name of pirated collections of "funny sayings." The *Jumping Frog* book, first of his own publications, had wide vogue with a varied class of readers. So general, in fact, was the curiosity about the author come out of the West that from the time when, as he said, he "stumbled into literature," in 1867, until the posthumous appearance of *The Mysterious Stranger* in 1916, indeed until the present time, a many-sided question concerning the status of Samuel Langhorne Clemens has intrigued the world. "How many sheep has Mark Twain? " his Arab guide asked of Richard Watson Gilder on the pyramid of Gizeh.

A review of the criticism called forth by the publication of his writings shows that the question has come from two main angles. The earlier critics apparently felt themselves to be attempting an answer to the inquiry, "What title has this fun-maker to be considered a legitimate author?" Later, after the publication of the Albert Bigelow Paine biography in 1912, and of *The Mysterious Stranger* in 1916, the question became a psychological rather than a purely literary one: "Given so arresting a mind and personality, how is it to be accounted for?"

From *Mark Twain: Son of Missouri* (Chapel Hill: Univ. of North Carolina Press), 1934, pp. 3-4.

MARK VAN DOREN: 1935

An Artist of Exaggeration

IT IS not enough to say of him that his humor consisted in exaggeration. His whole art consisted in that, and his only art. There was nothing else that he knew how to do with an absolute perfection. He did not think far, even if he thought clearly; he was often deficient in taste; he could be outrageously sentimental; he was in many respects an ignorant man, and could be in turn too proud and too apologetic about this ignorance. But whenever, as frequently happened, he got going about something, it was more than likely that he would develop the speed and the beauty and the form by which we have learned to recognize him at his height. At such moments and in such passages he was possessed by that ancient and noble thing, poetic rage. It possessed him at the same time that he controlled it for the purposes of his peculiar art. He mounted through his theme with an incredible celerity, riding the fieriest steeds known to rhetoric, and the broadest-winged—iteration, reiteration, and multiplied example. He mounted with gigantic ease and a vast naturalness, reaching the top of his subject at last and breathing the great air there with happy lungs; then suddenly descended to the ground and jogged along to the next inspiration. Or, to change the metaphor, he blew a bag up till it almost burst; at his best he did not let it burst, but tossed it lightly away and left it floating. Or, to change the metaphor once more, his prose was a river which regularly widened its banks, swelling and accelerating until there was danger that it should cease to look like a river; when it subsided and narrowed again, pulling us onward to new bays.

From "A Century of Mark Twain," *The Nation,* 141 (October 23, 1935), 473.

A. H. QUINN: 1936

Twain's Distinguishing Qualities

CERTAIN QUALITIES in Mark Twain lifted him out of the category of the professional humorists who flourished during his early period, men like Artemus Ward, Josh Billings, or Bill Nye, who are now practically forgotten. Mark Twain never allowed himself to be taken merely as a "funny man." Although he said in *Following the Equator,* "I have never been able to tell lies anybody would doubt or a truth anybody would believe," yet his sincere love of justice and his wide sympathy forced recognition of other phases of his work than his fun-making and saved him from being considered merely as a joker. He never descended to bad spelling and eccentricities to attract attention, and while he sacrificed immediate laughter, he won thereby an universal appeal. This quality of Mark Twain has carried his work abroad and made him a world artist.

But it was, after all, his ability to create character and his gift of narrative which distinguished him most clearly from the other humorists. While it is impossible to accept his statement in the *Literary Essays* that "the humorous story is American, the comic story is English and the witty story is French," his definition of the humorous story as one that "may be spun out to great length and may wander about as much as it pleases, and arrive nowhere in particular" is illuminating in its explanation of his strength and his weakness as a writer of fiction. Like Bret Harte he is best in his episodes, and it is through them that he built up the characters of Tom Sawyer, Huck Finn, Colonel Sellers, Tom Canty, Joan of Arc, those by which he will be best remembered. All but Colonel Sellers were under eighteen years of age.

He helped the cause of realism by his faithful representation of a civilization in Missouri which he knew; but, notwithstanding his denunciations of Scott and Cooper, he was really at home in a land of romance, and he could lead his readers into it best through the heart of a boy, whether that boy dreamt on the banks of the Mississippi of the mighty river flowing past him, or had visions in his den in Offal Court of the splendors of a princely castle. His wife's name for him, "Youth," reveals her thorough understanding of his nature. It was not because he failed to mature, however, but because he never grew old, that Mark Twain's fiction retains its vitality and makes its perennial appeal.

When he died in 1910 he left as definite an impression as any American writer of his generation. But the spontaneous and almost world-wide tributes during his centenary in 1935 were paid not so much to the novelist as to the great humorist who had added so largely to the joy of mankind.

From *American Fiction: An Historical and Critical Survey* (New York: Appleton-Century, 1936), pp. 255-56.

Critics on Twain since 1940

FLOYD STOVALL: 1943

"His Charm and His Weakness"

WHATEVER DEDUCTIONS must be made from Mark Twain's satire on the materialism of the Gilded Age, the sincerity of his attacks on its sentimentality is beyond question. He hated its simpering and sniveling, and he hated its self-abasement before Europe. . . .

Mark Twain was not altogether free of sentimentality himself, as we may observe in his essay "In Defense of Harriet Shelley," where he is guilty of the very sins of which he accuses Shelley's biographers. His sincere admiration of Joan of Arc is evidence that there were even some things medieval that he could accept like a devotee. He was a man of many contradictions, and he was governed more by his emotions than by his rational mind. In short, he was a representative American of his time, whether of East or West, and illustrated the faults as well as the virtues of his fellow countrymen. Like them he was a lover of plots and adventures, of wild exaggeration and practical jokes, of natural wonders and mechanical ingenuities; like them too he was ignorant, cynical, and crude, but withal naïvely sincere and magnanimous. He was a typical adolescent: that was the source of his charm and his weakness.

From *American Idealism* (Norman: Univ. of Oklahoma Press, 1943), pp. 114-15.

ALEXANDER COWIE: 1948

"Excited Ignorance"

MARK TWAIN once said of himself that he lived constantly in a state of "excited ignorance." His customary exaggeration marks the phrase, but it is accurate in its suggestion of how little, comparatively, he learned from orthodox books. Schooling was a minor element of his boyhood, and college he knew chiefly as the recipient of a number of honorary degrees. Latin and Greek writers were unthought of. French was a difficult language with which he wrestled manfully during the composition of *Joan of Arc.*[1] Italian was a vehicle for ordering food and arguing with hotel-keepers and cabmen. German (which Mark Twain knew best of the foreign languages) was a ridiculously involved jargon whose quaint syntax obsessed him; it was not the door to the works of Goethe and Schiller. Book-learning was not his passion. To Mark Twain, the itinerant printer, the miner, the pilot, and the lecturer, books were for spare time, and even as such they came second to storytelling for real diversion. To Mark Twain, the successful author, they were unnecessary. To Mark Twain, the inveterate billiard-player, they were a comparatively dull substitute for real fun. In any case a man so restless physically that he could scarcely sit through a meal without jumping up at least once to pace the floor in eager recitation or argument was not likely to be contented for very long with a book. Outside of working hours Mark Twain was "on the go." In his study he was writing. There was evidently much truth in Howells' observation that of all the writers he had known Mark Twain was "the most unliterary in his make and manner."[2]

From *The Rise of the American Novel* (New York: American Book, 1948), pp. 640-41.

1. French he must have begun early, for he amused himself by translating his *Jumping Frog of Calaveras County* (1867) into it—only to "claw" it back into English at once.
2. *My Mark Twain,* p. 17. Mark Twain probably did not have a really wide familiarity with books. Pilots on the river regarded him as a "great reader" (A.B. Paine, *Mark Twain: A Biography,* New York: Harper & Brothers, 1912, I, 151), but such a reputation was too easily secured to be significant. Rather impressive data on his reading have been compiled by scholars. Yet in a life-time of seventy years a man must read *something.* His biographer's testimony is that he "read not so many books ... but read a few books often." (Quoted in Edward Wagenknecht, *Mark Twain: The Man and His Work,* New Haven: Yale University Press, 1935, p. 46.)

GLADYS C. BELLAMY: 1950

Twain's Pessimism

CRITICS HAVE found it difficult to explain why Mark Twain—a man of genius, fame, wealth, happy domestic relations, and pleasant social environment—should have become a pessimist. He did not, in fact, become a pessimist, for pessimism flares out occasionally even in his early work. Surely, from an external view, life had brought him all that he could have hoped for. He had proved that a man might go just as far in America as his own talent and energy would take him. But he recoiled from the spiritual ugliness that grew up in the country in the years following the Civil War. Some of it escaped him, but what he had the vision to see he excoriated with force and power. His indictment of civilization is both explicit and implicit in his work. He was one of the first writers to sense what lay ahead of the United States in the course on which she was set. And, because to him America had long embodied the hope of the world, his fear and despair were for all the world. America as a democracy amid certain social conditions, under certain dominant factors of economics, politics, and religion, and the life he lived in such a setting—these elements make up the background. The foreground must remain his works themselves.

From *Mark Twain as a Literary Artist* (Norman: Univ. of Oklahoma Press, 1950), p. 25.

HENRY S. CANBY: 1951

A "Treasure" in Hannibal

MARK, as he grew more creative, was driven back upon his early youth both by predilection and inability to nourish his imagination from the contemporary scene. He could satirize it; he could not make it live. His new friends, his new interests, his new environment satisfied him deeply, but did not stimulate his extraordinary faculty for recreating life. This life had to be young in order to be felt, for he was young regardless of age—and to be young it had to be retrospective, rising from the memory. In the rich material of his reporter's books on the West and the River, there were brilliant glimpses of his power to make personality and invent fictious incident. But back of and deeper, more mellowed, more taken into the depths of the consciousness, lay the most intense life of all—the sensitive years of his first adventures into the glamour and excitement of a free life on his own, in what seemed an illimitable world of promise. Then this fortunate American boy was growing up in the morning time of the West, in a boy's realistic Heaven, even though aspects of Hell and Purgatory lay beneath his innocent bare feet.

From *Turn West, Turn East—Mark Twain and Henry James* (Boston: Houghton Mifflin, 1951), p. 131.

ROBERT E. SPILLER: 1955

Variety, Range, Power

THE FIRST major American author to be born west of the Mississippi, Mark Twain *was* what Walt Whitman talked about and what Howells described. Whether a child who never grew up, as one critic believes, or a genius whose very faults are his virtues, as another would argue, this son of the heartland came to symbolize the variety and range and power of the American spirit. The Mississippi was his bloodstream and his hands reached across two oceans. The incurable optimism and humor of the frontier were written into his earliest work, and the dark dismay of its failure into his latest. Responsive to every fact and mood of his time and place, Mark Twain was the artist of the folk, the teller of the tales that make a people. Unconscious of the larger meanings that his own best works convey, he gave to others the perspective that he could never quite define for himself. His art was natural, organic, wholly valid. Always it was the voice of a people; at its best it was epic.

From *The Cycle of American Literature: An Essay in Historical Criticism* (New York: Macmillan, 1955), pp. 150-51.

The "Journalist's Instinct" and Twain as Novelist

MARK TWAIN does not strive to be an artist—*artiste*, he probably would have called it with a grin. He would have felt more comfortable wearing the term journalist. He grew up a journalist, like Dickens, and was one of those hearty nineteenth-century scribblers who strayed into literature almost without realizing it. He had the journalist's instinct, in the way Defoe had, and in the way Hawthorne and James did not. This is not necessarily a handicap in the creation of literature. In so far as it stimulates a sense of audience, a sense of common scene, and the use of native speech and lore—in so far, that is, that it inspires one to attempt a colloquy in common terms but with uncommon genius, it is a definite and rare gift. Its limitations are likely to be great also, the limitations of the known, and especially what is known to the particular group. Mark Twain's writing was almost always a means to an end. He had few impersonal objectives in mind in the way of form, experiment, texture, design. He had the common touch and knew it was a blessing. He was enriched by it and made world-famous. . . .

One of the first things we can say about Mark Twain as a novelist is that he did not regard novel-writing as his essential "calling"—in the way that Flaubert, James, Mann, Dostoyevsky, Faulkner, Hemingway and other writers did. Mark Twain came to novel-writing almost accidentally and did not give to it the major part of his literary energy. He did not *begin* as a novelist. He wrote his first novel, *The Gilded Age,* only after he had poured out a great deal of literary energy on his first two books of non-fiction, *The Innocents Abroad* and *Roughing It.* And when he did begin, he began as only a half-novelist, inasmuch as he co-authored *The Gilded Age* with Charles Dudley Warner. *The Gilded Age* was conceived, as we shall see, not only as a sort of accident but as a kind of joke as well.

Few great novelists have had such an inauspicious beginning, and the history of the novel does not reveal for us many prominent examples of co-authorship. But if Mark Twain was eccentric in his beginnings as a novelist it should not surprise us. He had a reputation in his day for being eccentric which he thoroughly enjoyed and encouraged. And if his beginnings were, shall we say, weak, that should not surprise us either, for if he lacked any great instinct as a novelist it was that instinct which we call the artistic conscience. Mark Twain did not hesitate to take liberties in his novels, and in his fiction in general, which he would have hesitated to take in his non-fiction. He had a respect for non-fiction which he often seemed to lack for fiction. He told Rudyard Kipling in 1890, "I never read novels myself except when the popular persecution forces me to—when people plague me to know what I think of the last book that everyone is reading. . . . Personally I never care for fiction or story books. What I like to read about are facts and statistics of any kind. If they are only facts about the raising of radishes they interest me." Clemens regarded himself from first to last as a reporter who had clear and quite stern responsibilities to his public, whatever the jigs and high kicks he performed in an overflow of good spirits, health and a desire to amuse. He thought of himself as an entertainer, but as a serious one; and, as he said in his last years in his autobiography, his humor was only incidental to his purpose—if it came, good, if not, it could be dispensed with, for he was concerned primarily with discussing a moral.

From *Mark Twain* (New York: Horizon Press, 1967), pp. 1-2, 183.

FRANK BALDANZA: 1961

The Mark Twain Figure

THE MARK TWAIN characteristics, however, settle into a blend of those personal traits of Clemens (now including, with some judicious expurgations, even the nastier tastes of Mr. Brown) which are consonant with the public figure he wants to present.

The Mark Twain figure is by-and-large a naive, incompetent lazy shirker, the one who rides in the wagon when the others walk, or who steers the boat instead of rowing it. When he does exercise a skill, such as in his piloting days, it is one dependent on keenness and sensitivity of observation and memory. It is also, incidentally, a position of glory that feeds his large vanity. His great projects of claiming timber land on Lake Tahoe or mining silver or tracking the mysterious Mr. Whiteman to his fabulously rich "cement mine" always end up in a loafing and fishing expedition. In his lack of practical skills, such as tying up a pack horse, he is always the drone and the parasite of the group. But he loves to talk and to listen (and, with somewhat reduced enthusiasm, to write). When he accidentally starts a ruinous forest fire, he calmly uses it for several paragraphs of purple prose.

As Clemens himself ages, the figure of Mark Twain changes little. During his travels in Germany, Switzerland, Australia, and India there is a dulling of the sense of pristine adventure; in its place, one more often finds the *longueurs* of the raconteur.

He is a keen observer who exercises a tender sense of justice on the phenomena he sees. He is, heart and soul, a prevaricator who plays with reality as does a child with a hunk of clay—flattening, lumping, stretching, and tearing it at will until it assumes an outrageous shape. The sum of these characteristics is an organically whole personality, in which the vanity does not prevent his admitting to substantial weaknesses, or in which the weaknesses do not cripple his sense of his own worth. The prevarication, however, is the nucleus of the whole organism; it is the looseness of his sense of accuracy which permits Clemens to project this lovable and genial personality of Mark Twain into the books. It is no accident, of course, that the laziness, impracticality, cowardice, and other such weaknesses are characteristic of most humorists' pseudonymous or artistically projected personalities—for instance Robert Benchley or James Thurber in our own day. The humorist in this sense continues the role of the medieval jester, a person whose life work is to profess human weakness, but, by warming it in his heart, to make of it a human triumph.

From *Mark Twain: An Introduction and Interpretation* (New York: Barnes & Noble, 1961), pp. 26-27.

EDWARD WAGENKNECHT: 1961

Twain's Use of Imagination

WHETHER MARK TWAIN got more material from literature or from life, there would seem to be no question that the material he got from life was the more vital. What he got from books was equally useful, but he could not use it until after it had been vitalized by his experience; his experience provided him with the means of making it seem real. Life vitalized literature; literature did not simply provide a means of escape from life, as is the case with later writers. As he grew older, his memory relinquished its hold on facts, but it retained impressions tenaciously. He may have stretched it a little when he described Tom Sawyer as belonging "to the composite order of architecture," but there are many things in his books which do belong to that order. So the last word belonged neither to reading nor to experience but to imagination. If he made himself Goldsmith and his mother Mrs. Partington, he altered what he saw and experienced no less freely than what he had read. The St. Petersburg of *Tom Sawyer* and *Huckleberry Finn* is not Hannibal; it is a created town that has grown out of Hannibal, and the alterations made by Mark Twain have been determined by his artistic purposes. In his pages Mississippi steamboating moves away from cutthroat competition and becomes an idyll. The original of Widow Douglas was a woman of Hannibal, but the Widow Douglas is a much lovelier person than her prototype had been. In life, Injun Joe did not die in the cave, though he was lost there on one occasion, and Huck Finn's refusal to surrender Jim was based upon a very different set of circumstances in the life of Tom Blankenship.

"The ancients stole our best thoughts," and Mark Twain's originality was the only kind that is possible for a modern writer. His art was the art that conceals art. As he himself once observed, "Shakespeare took other people's quartz and extracted the gold from it—it was a nearly valueless commodity before."

From *Mark Twain: The Man and His Work,* rev. ed. (Norman: Univ. of Oklahoma Press, 1961), pp. 67-68.

PASCAL COVICI, JR.: 1962

Beyond Humor

ALTHOUGH MARK TWAIN'S writing draws upon the traditions and materials utilized by earlier southwestern humorists, its humor goes beyond an exposure of deliberate affectation. In psychological awareness, Twain is closely akin to Melville and Henry James, for he presents human beings as more disposed to misunderstand themselves, as do Pierre and the first-person protagonists of *The Turn of the Screw* and *The Sacred Fount,* than to mislead others deliberately. Consequently, his technique, his literary organization of material, is more concerned with laying bare the human heart than with presenting the rogue's world as it was at a given time and place. Anyone who reads carefully the introduction to the king's camp meeting cannot help but be impressed by the meticulous acuteness of the description, even down to the benches "made out of outside slabs of logs, with holes bored in the round side to drive sticks into for legs" (XIII, 181). To say that Twain is not concerned at all with the surface appearance of the life surrounding his characters is clearly to overstate the point. It is his particular use of appearances that sets him off from his humorous predecessors.

From *Mark Twain's Humor: The Image of a World* (Dallas: Southern Methodist Univ. Press, 1962), pp. 19-20.

Master of the Vernacular

MARK TWAIN converted the American vernacular into a subtle literary instrument equal to the most arduous demands the literary artist could put upon it. As Walter Blair said, the talk of his characters "had the precision, the imagination of poetic art,"[1] and in the nineties *Huckleberry Finn* was already quietly advancing toward the position that it would enjoy among writers of the twentieth century, a position most dramatically stated by Ernest Hemingway when he said: "It's the best book we've had. All American writing comes from that. There was nothing before. There has been nothing as good since."[2]

> From *The American 1890s: Life and Times of a Lost Generation* (New York: Viking, 1966), pp. 67-68.

1. *Native American Humor* (New York: American Book Company, 1937), p. 162.
2. *Green Hills of Africa* (New York: Charles Scribner's Sons, 1935), p. 22.

ALLISON ENSOR: 1969

The New View

THE PRESENT GENERATION has discovered a new Mark Twain. No longer is he merely the nostalgic recaller of the past, the teller of tall tales, the producer of humorous quips. No one today would describe him in the terms used by Stuart P. Sherman in his sketch for the *Cambridge History of American Literature:* "Mark Twain is one of our great representative men. He is a fulfilled promise of American life. He proves the virtues of the land and the society in which he was born and fostered. He incarnates the spirit of an epoch of American history when the nation . . . entered lustily upon new adventures."[1] Thanks to the posthumous publication of a number of his own works and to the efforts of the many scholars who have directed their attention toward him, we now know that he was a far more complex figure, a man divided against himself almost as much as his "extraordinary twins" whose bedtime reading consisted of *The Age of Reason* and *The Whole Duty of Man.*

From *Mark Twain & the Bible* (Lexington: Univ. Press of Kentucky, 1969), p. 94.

1. (New York, 1918-1921), III, 1.

MAXWELL GEISMAR: 1970

The Triumph of the Later Period

⌈HE ENTERED his mature and later periods of writing quite triumphantly indeed, with all his old powers enhanced, rather than broken or diminished,⌋ by his own central tragic experience; by his depth realization of life's pain and evil. He retained to the end the central source of his artistic virtue: that untouched spring of pagan, plenary, and edenic innocence, that full sense of joy and pleasure in life, which sprang up even more freely in his final decades—which came to a second and later flowering despite all those civilizational discontents which he, perhaps more than any other American writer, also felt so directly and personally at the center of his being.

It was only certain Twain critics, from the youthful Van Wyck Brooks, who came to change his mind, to Bernard De Voto and Charles Neider and Justin Kaplan, as we've seen, who refused to acknowledge—or who were perhaps ignorant of—the value of his later writing. Mark Twain was more correct in his own estimate of that work, his joy in writing it, and yes, his pleasure in receiving the world's acclamation then (and yet again today) for having written it.⌈The last periods of his writing were indeed younger in spirit if wiser in essence than much of his earlier and middle periods of work.⌋ *Huck Finn* as his single great classic—what nonsense! His whole career was a classic. He was not merely the artist of American youth and the past; he was surely our most mature and wisest of artists whose acerbity and profundity alike were ringed about with the imperishable comic spirit.⌈In his age he only became freer, bolder, more open and honest, more emancipated both socially and sexually, from the taboos of his epoch which, at base, his spirit had never accepted.⌋

From *Mark Twain: An American Prophet* (Boston: Houghton Mifflin, 1970), pp. 535-36.

General Critical Evaluations

ROBERT M. GAY

The Two Mark Twains

THE HISTORY of Mark Twain's reputation is a curious one, and in some ways exasperating to his lovers. A perverse fate has pursued it. Ever since his greater works appeared, opinion about him has flown off at tangents, until it seemed as if he never would receive a sober appraisal. At one time it was his morality that was questioned; at another, his taste; at a third, his spiritual honesty. He was accepted by the great public as a mere jester, and by the critics was used as an example to illustrate critical theories. Thousands of pages were covered in showing what he was not, but hardly ever did anyone try to show what he really was. The reason was partly that there were two Mark Twains: one, the man I have called the rhetorician; the other, one whom we may call the poet. The former was showy, obvious, and delightful, but hardly competent to win a position as a great writer. The latter was often hidden behind the jester and showman, and was sometimes, even in his best work, in abeyance.

Perhaps the showman was diffident about the poet, afraid of his tenderness, wistfulness, and human sympathy. Strength is always afraid that sentiment is effeminate, and the realist in Mark Twain was never quite at ease with the dreamer. When he relied on his intuitions he was nearly always right and true, and instinctively he was a lover of his kind. But he hardly ever expressed this love without self-consciousness except when he was viewing the world through the somewhat nostalgic atmosphere that surrounded his boyhood memories. In *Mark Twain in Eruption* it is a little pathetic to see how, the moment his mind goes back far enough, his style kindles, his smartness disappears, charm suffuses the most trivial incident.

I wonder whether his later critics have not mistaken what was really the matter with him in his old age. They have assumed that he became cynical and pessimistic. But he always was so. His mind always told him that life was bad. But his feelings told him that it was good, and as long as his feelings had fuel to burn, as long as they were engaged with affections formed before he became a thinking being, he could safely let them be. All his life he had a good and a bad angel at his two shoulders; there is nothing new in the melancholy of the Autobiography—only, the time came when he had used all the memories about which his good angel could sing and was left only with later impressions about which his bad angel could prose or snarl.

In this he is really not different from other men. The Greeks made poetry the daughter of Memory; and perhaps the myth suggests the reason why so many great novelists have written their masterpiece about the memories of their youth.

If I can trust my own memory, the popular view of Mark Twain before the turn of the century was that he was a writer of excruciatingly funny stories and of books for children. Of the latter, two—*The Prince and the Pauper* and *Joan of Arc*—were quite safe reading for children, but two others,—*Tom Sawyer* and *Huckleberry Finn,*—though no doubt very amusing, were far too rowdy for nice little boys and girls. It is hard for me to believe that *Tom Sawyer* was published before I was born and *Huckleberry Finn* when I was five years old, because I certainly never read them until I had grown up. In our provincial neighborhood Mark Twain was a familiar name all through my boyhood, because many of his sketches—no doubt his worst—were favorites with parlor elocutionists; but my own lack of acquaintance with his masterpieces suggests that they were carefully kept out of my reach.

My elders no doubt thought they were protecting my taste and morals, and I cannot believe that they were unique or even unusual in this. Van Wyck Brooks records that the books were excluded from the public libraries of my home town. I certainly remember that some of my playmates were reading *Huckleberry Finn* secretly in the attic.

It is possible that the general public ran true to form in liking the worst books best; but this hardly accounts for the slowness of the professional critics and literary historians to recognize that *Tom Sawyer, Life on the Mississippi,* and *Huckleberry Finn* were national masterpieces. Reasons can be assigned, the main one being critical inertia and timidity. Gradually, nevertheless, the realization came that Mark Twain was one of our great writers, whom it was not extravagant to compare with Dickens, Molière, Dumas, and Cervantes. These comparisons really were made, though somewhat casually, before he attained, in the nineteen-twenties, a vogue among the intellectuals.

In that peculiar decade he became the centre of a controversy which tended further to postpone a final estimate of his quality. Everyone remembers it, I suppose, and it has not even yet entirely subsided. It began when the cult of the frontier or Middle West found in him a handy example of a product strictly made-in-America. It was only a step to the conclusion that his history presented a parable of the distressful condition of the artist in America. This theory found an eloquent advocate in Van Wyck Brooks and a pugnacious opponent in Bernard De Voto. The fallacy in the theory was perhaps natural to intellectuals: it treated Mark Twain as if he were an intellectual. But if there was ever an intuitionalist it was he. He was so creative that whenever he attempted philosophic thought he seemed like a great, solemn, lovable baby. His at times astonishing insight and wisdom were the fruit, not of philosophy, but of human sympathy. His illuminations came through his feelings.

Has not the time come to continue the work laid out by De Voto in *Mark Twain's America?* To reëxamine the works, not for what they lack, but for what they have? Concerning his greatest work, nearly everybody is now agreed that it has exuberance of vitality. Like all great fiction, it has a positively therapeutic power, not only because it contains the great cure-all, laughter, but because it is so completely sane. This sanity, which shows as a balance of laughter and tears, of observation and imagination, of thought and feeling, is found only in a few writers, and these of the greatest.

From *Atlantic Monthly,* 165 (December 1940), 725-26.

F. L. PATTEE

Twain the Romancer

THERE ARE three Mark Twains: there is Mark Twain, the droll comedian, who wrote for the masses and made them laugh; there is Mark Twain, the indignant protester, who arose ever and anon to true eloquence in his denunciation of tyranny and pretense; and there is Mark Twain, the romancer, who in his boyhood had dreamed by the great river and who later caught the romance of a period in American life. The masterpiece of the first is *The Jumping Frog*, of the second *The Man that Corrupted Hadleyburg*, and of the third *Life on the Mississippi* and *Roughing It*.

It is this third Mark Twain that still lives and that will continue to live in American literature. He saw with distinctness a unique area of American life. As the brief and picturesque era faded away he caught the sunset glory of it and embodied it in romance—the steamboat days on the river in the slavery era, the old régime in the South, the barbarism of the Plains, the great buffalo herds, the wild camps in the gold fields of Nevada and California. In half a dozen books: *Roughing It, Life on the Mississippi, the Gilded Age* (a few chapters of it), *Tom Sawyer, Huckleberry Finn, Pudd'nhead Wilson*, he has done work that can never be done again. The world that these books depict has vanished as completely as the Bagdad of Haroun al Raschid. Not only has he told the story of this vanished world, illustrating it with descriptions and characterizations that are like Flemish portraits, but he has caught and held the spirit of it, and he has thrown over it all the nameless glow of romance. It is as golden a land that he leads us through as any we may find in Scott, and yet it was drawn from the life with painstaking care. Scott and Bulwer and Cooper angered Mark Twain. They were careless of facts, they were sentimental, they misinterpreted the spirit of the times they depicted and the men and women who lived in them, but these six books of Mark Twain may be placed among the source books of American history. Nowhere else can one catch so truly certain phases of the spirit of the mid-nineteenth century West. Over every page of them may be written those words from the preface of *The Innocents Abroad*, "I am sure I have written at least honestly, whether wisely or not."

The books are six chapters of autobiography. *Tom Sawyer* and *Huckleberry Finn* are recollections of that boyhood by the river after so long a time had elapsed that the day-dreams and boyish imaginings were recorded as real happenings; *Life on the Mississippi* records that romantic adventure of his young manhood as he recalled it in later days when the old piloting era had vanished like a dream of boyhood; *The Gilded Age,* a book of glorious fragments, has in it his uncle James Lampton drawn from life and renamed Colonel Sellers; *Roughing It* bubbles over with the joy and the high spirits and the excitement of those marvelous days when the author and the West were young together; and *Pudd'nhead Wilson* gives the tragedy of slavery as it passed before his boyish eyes. These books and *The Innocents Abroad* are Mark Twain's contribution to the library of American classics. The rest of his enormously large output, despite brilliant passages here and there, does not greatly matter.

They are not artistic books. The author had little skill in construction. He excelled in brilliant dashes, not in long-continued effort. He was his own Colonel Sellers, restless, idealistic, Quixotic. What he did he did with his whole soul without restraint or sense of proportion. There is in all he wrote a lack of refinement, kept at a minimum, to be sure, by his wife, who for years was his editor and severest critic, but likely at any moment to crop out. His books, all of them, are monotones, a running series of episodes and descriptions all of the same value, never reaching dramatic climax. The episodes themselves, however, are told with graphic intensity; some of them are gems well-nigh perfect. Here is a picture of the famous pony express of the Plains:

> The pony-rider was usually a little bit of a man, brimful of spirit and endurance. No matter what time of the day or night his watch came on, and no matter whether it was winter or summer, raining, snowing, hailing, or sleeting, or whether his "beat" was a level straight road or a crazy trail over mountain crags and precipices, or whether it led through peaceful regions that swarmed with hostile Indians, he must be always ready to leap into the saddle and be off like the wind. He rode fifty miles without stopping, by daylight, moonlight, starlight, or through the blackness of darkness—just as it happened. He rode a splendid horse that was born for a racer and fed and lodged like a gentleman; kept him at his utmost speed for ten miles, and then, as he came crashing up to the station where stood two men holding fast a fresh, impatient steed, the transfer of rider and mailbag was made in the twinkling of an eye, and away flew the eager pair and were out of sight before the spectator could hardly get the ghost of a look.
>
> We had had a consuming desire, from the beginning, to see a pony-rider, but somehow or other all that had passed us and all that met us managed to streak by in the night, and so we heard only a whiz and a hail, and the swift phantom of the desert was

gone before we could get our heads out of the windows. But now we were expecting one along every moment, and we would see him in broad daylight. Presently the driver exclaims:

"Here he comes!"

Every neck is stretched further, and every eye strained wider. Away across the endless dead level of the prairie a black speck appears against the sky, and it is plain that it moves. Well, I should think so! In a second or two it becomes a horse and rider, rising and falling, rising and falling—sweeping toward us nearer and nearer—growing more and more distinct, more and more sharply defined—nearer and still nearer, and the flutter of the hoofs comes faintly to the ear—another instant a whoop and a hurrah from our upper deck, a wave of the rider's hand, but no reply, and man and horse burst past our excited faces, and go winging away like a belated fragment of a storm.

The steamboat race and the explosion in chapter four of *The Gilded Age* have few equals in any language for mere picturing power. He deals largely with the out-of-doors. His canvases are bounded only by the horizon: the Mississippi, the great Plains, the Rocky Mountains, Mono Lake, the Alkali Deserts, and the Sierras—he has handled a continent. Only Joaquin Miller and John Muir have used canvases as vast. Huckleberry Finn's floating journey down the river on his raft has in it something of the spirit of *The Odyssey* and *Pilgrim's Progress* and *Don Quixote*. Had Mark Twain's constructive skill and his ability to trace the growth of a human soul been equal to his picturing power, his Defoelike command of detail and situation, and his mastery of phrase and of narrative, he might have said the last word in American fiction. He was a product of his section and of his education. College and university would have made of him an artist like Holmes, brilliant, refined, and messageless. It would have robbed him of the very fountain-head of his power. It was his to work not from books but from life itself, to teach truth and genuineness of life, to turn the eyes of America from the romance of Europe to her own romantic past.

From *A History of American Literature Since 1870* (New York: Century, 1915), pp. 58-61.

CARL VAN DOREN

Mark Twain

OF THE MAJOR American novelists Mark Twain, who hardly thought of himself as a novelist at all, derived least from any literary, or at any rate from any bookish, tradition. Hawthorne had the example of Irving, and Cooper had that of Scott, when they began to write; Howells and Henry James instinctively fell into step with classics. Mark Twain came up into literature from the popular ranks, trained in the school of newspaper fun-making and humorous lecturing, only gradually instructed in the more orthodox arts of the literary profession. He seems, however, less indebted to predecessors than he actually was, for the reason that his provenience has faded out with the passage of time and the increase of his particular fame. Yet he had predecessors and a provenience. As a printer he learned the mechanical technique of his trade of letters; as a jocose writer for the newspapers of the Middle West and the Far West at a period when a well established mode of exaggeration and burlesque and caricature and dialect prevailed there, he adapted himself to a definite convention; as a raconteur he not only tried his methods on the most diverse auditors but consciously studied those of Artemus Ward, then the American master of the craft; Bret Harte, according to Mark Twain, "trimmed and trained and schooled me"; and thereafter, when the Wild Humorist of the Pacific Slope, as it did not at first seem violent to call him, came into contact with professed men of letters, especially Howells, he had already a mastership of his own.

To be a humorist in the United States of the sixties and seventies was to belong to an understood and accepted class. It meant, as Orpheus C. Kerr and John Phoenix and Josh Billings and Petroleum V. Nasby and Artemus Ward had recently and typically been showing, to make fun as fantastically as one liked but never to rise to beauty; to be intensely shrewd but very seldom profound; to touch pathos at intervals but not tragedy. The humorist assumed a name not his own, as Mark Twain did, and also generally a character: that of some rustic sage or adventurous eccentric who discussed the topics of the moment keenly and drolly. Under his assumed character, of which he ordinarily made fun, he claimed a wide license of speech, which did not extend to indecency or to any too serious satire. His fun was the ebullience of a strenuous society, the laughter of escape from difficult conditions. It was rooted fast in that optimism which Americans have had the habit of considering a moral obligation. It loved to ridicule those things which to the general public seemed obstacles to the victorious progress of an average democracy; it laughed about equally at idlers and idealists, at fools and poets, at unsuccessful sinners and unsuccessful saints. It could take this attitude toward minorities because it was so confident of having the great American majority at its back, hearty, kindly, fair-intentioned, but self-satisfied and unspeculative. In time Mark Twain largely outgrew this type of fun—or rather, had longer and longer intervals of a different type and also of a fierce seriousness—but the origins of his art lie there. So do the origins of his ideas lie among the populace, much as he eventually outgrew of the evangelical orthodoxy and national complacency and personal hopefulness with which he had first been furnished. The secret alike of his powers and of his limitations must be looked for in the dual, the never quite completed, nature which allowed him on one side to touch, say, Petroleum V. Nasby and on the other William Dean Howells. . . .

The art of Mark Twain springs hardly less truly than his ideas from the American people as a whole. "I like history, biography, travel, curious facts and strange happenings, and science," he said. "And I detest novels, poetry, and theology." He would have been the last to reflect in what category his own writing fell, and he never suspected that he would come in time to be thought of as having raised the frontier tall tale into literature. As to novelists, he could not stand Henry James or George Eliot or Hawthorne; he found Scott an unendurable snob and Cooper a literary bungler; he developed his loathing for Jane Austen until he came to take a positive delight in uttering it in the most violent language; and his admiration for the work of Howells must be assigned in part to his affection for the man. Mark Twain's taste lay wholly in the direction of large actions, large passions, large scenery. That he moved so casually over the face of the earth and through the historical periods he knew is proof enough that he possessed none of the professed realist's timidity when on unaccustomed ground. No Franklin ever felt more at home in ticklish surroundings than Mark Twain did. This same confidence, which deprived him of the austere seriousness of some men of letters, stood by him also in his methods. He did not mind a sudden change of key, but could fall from passionate eloquence to burlesque, and climb from farce to tragedy without even thinking whether this suited the dignity of literature. Though at times he seems to have respected academic judgment too much—especially as represented by Howells and the *Atlantic's* audience —and though he latterly resented the opinion that he was a humorist merely, he did depend in his art primarily upon the humorist's technique.

"To string incongruities and absurdities together in a wandering and sometimes purposeless way, and seem innocently unaware that they are absurdities, is the basis of the American art," he said of the oral method of humor. The tricks of oral delivery are those he used most, whether he spoke or wrote. His rapid improvisation has the effect of flowing speech. To all appearances—which are borne out by what is known of his habits of composition—he drove his pen through his sentences at almost the rate of conversation, and had constantly a physical audience in mind. On it he tried his "wandering and purposeless" incongruities, his "slurring of the point," his "dropping of a studied remark apparently without knowing it, apparently as if one were thinking aloud." When actually lecturing he could hold, with his inflections and pauses, the attention of the most fastidious hearers as well as of the ordinary crowd, making capital of his lower moments and shading down the higher with humorous deprecation. Even in the comparative coolness of print his methods were essentially oral. They reveal themselves in his partiality for autobiographical narrative, in his rambling sentence-structure, in his anti-climaxes and afterthoughts. Above all they are revealed in his humoristic device of occupying the stage so much of the time in his own person. For Mark Twain to practise his art was, more than with any other American writer, to exhibit and expound his own personality. The greatness of his personality was the measure of his fame.

Accepted from the first by the public, he was toward the end of his life recognized by universities, with honorary degrees from Yale (1901) and Oxford (1907), and after his death came to be a focus of criticism in an age which brought a new note into American literature. *Mark Twain* (1912), the authorized biography by Albert Bigelow Paine, and *Mark Twain's Letters* (1917) made his life nearly as well known as his work. Advanced criticism fixed upon him as a dark example of the danger of too much concession to the popular taste and of the repression of unpopular ideas in an artist. His career was cited as proof that the United States discouraged originality and candor. *Mark Twain's Autobiography* (1924) had a Preface as from the Grave in which he said: "I speak from the grave rather than with my living tongue, for a good reason: I can speak thence freely. . . . It has seemed to me that I could be as frank and free and unembarrassed as a love letter if I knew that what I was writing would be exposed to no eye till I was dead, and unaware, and indifferent." But the *Autobiography* itself seemed hardly so reckless as he had thought it. Though his sensitive conscience had accused him of playing safe, he had probably spoken out on most of the matters which most concerned him. He was not primarily a thinker, but rather a natural force which had moved through the world laughing, an American Adam with the eye of innocence giving new names to what he saw.

From *The American Novel, 1789-1939* (New York: Macmillan, 1940), pp. 137-38, 160-62.

EDWARD WAGENKNECHT

Some Classifications

MARK TWAIN is so incomparably the dominating personality in American literature, the mightiest figure in our American literary mythology, that one who would write about him as novelist merely must inevitably feel somewhat cabined, cribbed, confined. There is the same difficulty in being dispassionate about him as is in being dispassionate about Lincoln, and when Howells called him "the Lincoln of our literature," he struck out the most telling and illuminating phrase concerning him that has yet been coined. He was the product of the same Midwestern frontier that produced Lincoln; indeed, he himself *was* that frontier in literature as unmistakably as Lincoln was that frontier in world statesmanship.

The fundamental difficulty with people who still imagine that Mark Twain wanted to be Shelley—or Zola—is that they have failed to remember that Mark Twain inherited and fulfilled a tradition: he did not establish one. When he began his work, the frontier already existed as literature, literature of pretty poor quality, much of it, but literature notwithstanding. Mr. DeVoto has described it clearly—fantasy and realism side by side, burlesque and extravaganza closely connected with satire—and Mr. Meine has illustrated its quality in his *Tall Tales of the Southwest.*[1]

The whole thing hangs together beautifully; the picture is one, not many. The frontier humorist was essentially an improviser, a raconteur. At the outset, his art was oral, not written, a literature without letters, and it never wholly lost the insignia of its origin.[2] The raconteur, like the actor dramatizes his own personality; and the actor, alone among artists, uses his own body and soul as the instrument upon which he plays. Mark Twain's platform work was no accident, no by-blow; it was an essential expression of his art. Neither is it an accident that, though he wrote one of the very greatest novels in American literature, we should always think of him first and his books afterward. The only thing that could not have been safely prophesied was the vastness and grandeur of the soul he had to express. That was simply a piece of colossal good luck, for America and for the world.

Mr. DeVoto has said that Mark Twain was essentially a novelist. It would surprise him to hear it. He did not consider himself a novelist— "can't write a novel, for I lack the faculty"—and except for the works of W. D. Howells, he did not think he really enjoyed novels. Novelist in the Howells or Henry James sense, he certainly was not, and only in the solitary instance of *The Gilded Age,* written in collaboration, did he even attempt to be.

Yet he importantly enlarged the scope of American fiction. And it is always something of a problem to differentiate between his fiction and his factual writings. There is, for example, a good deal of fiction in his travel narratives, though they can scarcely fall for consideration in a history of the American novel. There might be some question, on the other hand, about such pieces as "The Man That Corrupted Hadleyburg" and "The $30,000 Bequest." Are they novels or short stories? My own working plan for the discussion of Mark Twain's fiction is as follows:

I.   FICTION OF THE CONTEMPORARY SCENE. *The Gilded Age,* with its pendant, *The American Claimant.*

II. FICTION OUT OF HANNIBAL. *The Adventures of Tom Sawyer* and *The Adventures of Huckleberry Finn,* with two addenda—*Tom Sawyer Abroad* and *Tom Sawyer, Detective; Pudd'nhead Wilson.*

III. HISTORY AND LEGEND. *The Prince and the Pauper, A Connecticut Yankee in King Arthur's Court, Personal Recollections of Joan of Arc, The Mysterious Stranger.*

That there is no overlapping here, I do not maintain. There is Mississippi folklore in both *Joan of Arc* and *The Mysterious Stranger,* and Joan's secretary, the Sieur Louis de Conte, sometimes speaks with the voice of Huck and Tom, which is Mark Twain's own voice. There is more of the nineteenth century than of the sixth in *A Connecticut Yankee.* Even as *The Mysterious Stranger* stands, Eseldorf is Hannibal with a medieval coloring, but in the first two (unpublished) versions of the story the coloring is absent; young Satan actually comes to Hannibal and associates with Huck and Tom. On the highest level of his creativity, Mark Twain never left the village where he grew up.

From *Cavalcade of the American Novel* (New York: Holt, Rinehart and Winston, 1952), pp. 114-16.

1. Franklin J. Meine, *Tall Tales of the Southwest* (K, 1930). See, also, Walter Blair, *Horse-Sense in American Humor* (UCP, 1942) and his anthology, *Native American Humor, 1800-1900* (ABC, 1937).

2. In her valuable *MT as a Literary Artist,* Miss Bellamy expresses a certain disagreement with this view, as previously expressed by myself, Constance Rourke, and other writers. But she and I are fundamentally in accord in our attitude toward Mark Twain, and I think I never intended, on this point, to be taken quite so literally as she shows some tendency to take me.

Critics on Specific Works

Introduction to *Huckleberry Finn*

The Adventures of Huckleberry Finn is the only one of Mark Twain's various books which can be called a masterpiece. I do not suggest that it is his only book of permanent interest; but it is the only one in which his genius is completely realized, and the only one which creates its own category. There are pages in *Tom Sawyer* and in *Life on the Mississippi* which are, within their limits, as good as anything with which one can compare them in *Huckleberry Finn;* and in other books there are drolleries just as good of their kind. But when we find one book by a prolific author which is very much superior to all the rest, we look for the peculiar accident or concourse of accidents which made that book possible. In the writing of *Huckleberry Finn* Mark Twain had two elements which, when treated with his sensibility and his experience, formed a great book: these two are the Boy and the River.

Huckleberry Finn is, no doubt, a book which boys enjoy. I cannot speak from memory: I suspect that a fear on the part of my parents lest I should acquire a premature taste for tobacco, and perhaps other habits of the hero of the story, kept the book out of my way. But *Huckleberry Finn* does not fall into the category of juvenile fiction. The opinion of my parents that it was a book unsuitable for boys left me, for most of my life, under the impression that it was a book suitable only for boys. Therefore it was only a few years ago that I read for the first time, and in that order, *Tom Sawyer* and *Huckleberry Finn.*

Tom Sawyer did not prepare me for what I was to find its sequel to be. *Tom Sawyer* seems to me to be a boys' book, and a very good one. The River and *the* Boy make their appearance in it; the narrative is good; and there is also a very good picture of society in a small mid-Western river town (for St. Petersburg is more Western than Southern) a hundred years ago. But the point of view of the narrator is that of an adult observing a boy. And Tom is the ordinary boy, though of quicker wits, and livelier imagination, than most. Tom is, I suppose, very much the boy that Mark Twain had been: he is remembered and described as he seemed to his elders, rather than created. Huck Finn, on the other hand, is the boy that Mark Twain still was, at the time of writing his adventures. We look at Tom as the smiling adult does: Huck we do not look at—we see the world through his eyes. The two boys are not merely different types; they were brought into existence by different processes. Hence in the second book their roles are altered. In the first book Huck is merely the humble friend—almost a variant of the traditional valet of comedy; and we see him as he is seen by the conventional respectable society to which Tom belongs, and of which, we feel sure, Tom will one day become an eminently respectable and conventional member. In the second book their nominal relationship remains the same; but here it is Tom who has the secondary role. The author was probably not conscious of this, when he wrote the first two chapters: *Huckleberry Finn* is not the kind of story in which the author knows, from the beginning, what is going to happen. Tom then disappears from our view; and when he returns, he has only two functions. The first is to provide a foil for Huck. Huck's persisting admiration for Tom only exhibits more clearly to our eyes the unique qualities of the former and the commonplaceness of the latter. Tom has the imagination of a lively boy who has read a good deal of romantic fiction: he might, of course, become a writer—he might become Mark Twain. Or rather, he might become the more commonplace aspect of Mark Twain. Huck has not imagination, in the sense in which Tom has it: he has, instead, vision. He sees the real world; and he does not judge it—he allows it to judge itself.

Tom Sawyer is an orphan. But he has his aunt; he has, as we learn later, other relatives; and he has the environment into which he fits. He is wholly a social being. When there is a secret band to be formed, it is Tom who organizes it and prescribes the rules. Huck Finn is alone: there is no more solitary character in fiction. The fact that he has a father only emphasizes his loneliness; and he views his father with a terrifying detachment. So we come to see Huck himself in the end as one of the permanent symbolic figures of fiction; but unworthy to take a place with Ulysses, Faust, Don Quixote, Don Juan, Hamlet and other great discoveries that man has made about himself.

It would seem that Mark Twain was a man who—perhaps like most of us—never became in all respects mature. We might even say that the adult side of him was boyish, and that only the boy in him, that was Huck Finn, was adult. As Tom Sawyer grown up, he wanted success and applause. (Tom himself always needs an audience). He wanted prosperity, a happy domestic life of a conventional kind, universal approval, and fame. All of these things he obtained. As Huck Finn he was indifferent to all these things; and being composite of the two, Mark Twain both strove for them, and resented their violation of his integrity. Hence he became the humorist and even clown: with his gifts, a certain way to success, for everyone could enjoy his writings without the slightest feeling of discomfort, self-consciousness or self-criticism. And hence, on the other hand, his pessimism and misanthropy. To be a misanthrope is to be in some way divided; or it is a sign of an uneasy conscience. The pessimism which Mark Twain discharged into *The Man That Corrupted Hadleyburg* and *What is Man?* springs less from observation of society, than from his hatred of himself for allowing society to tempt and corrupt him and give him what he wanted. There is no wisdom in it. But all this personal problem has been diligently examined by Mr. Van Wyck Brooks; and it is not Mark Twain, but *Huckleberry Finn*, that is the subject of this introduction.

You cannot say that Huck himself is either a humorist or a misanthrope. He is the impassive observer: he does not interfere, and, as I have said, he does not judge. Many of the episodes that occur on the voyage down the river, after he is joined by the Duke and the King (whose fancies about themselves are akin to the kind of fancy that Tom Sawyer enjoys) are in themselves farcical; and if it were not for the presence of Huck as the reporter of them, they would be no more than farce. But, seen through the eyes of Huck, there is a deep human pathos in these scoundrels. On the other hand, the story of the feud between the Grangerfords and the Shepherdsons is a masterpiece in itself: yet Mark Twain could not have written it so, with that economy and restraint, with just the right details and no more, and leaving to the reader to make his own moral reflections, unless he had been writing in the person of Huck. And the *style* of the book, which is the style of Huck, is what makes it a far more convincing indictment of slavery than the sensationalist propaganda of *Uncle Tom's Cabin*. Huck is passive and impassive, apparently always the victim of events; and yet, in his acceptance of his world and of what it does to him and others, he is more powerful than his world, because he is more *aware* than any other person in it.

Repeated readings of the book only confirm and deepen one's admiration of the consistency and perfect adaptation of the writing. This is a style which at the period, whether in America or in England, was an innovation, a new discovery in the English language. Other authors had achieved natural speech in relation to particular characters—Scott with characters talking Lowland Scots, Dickens with cockneys: but no one else had kept it up through the whole of a book. Thackeray's Yellowplush, impressive as he is, is an obvious artifice in comparison. In *Huckleberry Finn* there is no exaggeration of grammar or spelling or speech, there is no sentence or phrase to destroy the illusion that these are Huck's own words. It is not only in the way in which he tells his story, but in the details he remembers, that Huck is true to himself. There is, for instance, the description of the Grangerford interior as Huck sees it on his arrival; there is the list of the objects which Huck and Jim salvaged from the derelict house:

> We got an old tin lantern, and a butcher-knife without any handle, and a bran-new Barlow knife worth two bits in any store, and a lot

of tallow candles, and a tin candlestick, and a gourd, and a tin cup, and a ratty old bedquilt off the bed, and a reticule with needles and pins and beeswax and buttons and thread and all such truck in it, and a hatchet and some nails, and a fish-line as thick as my little finger, with some monstrous hooks on it, and a roll of buckskin, and a leather dog-collar, and a horseshoe, and some vials of medicine that didn't have no label on them; and just as we was leaving I found a tolerable good curry-comb, and Jim he found a ratty old fiddlebow, and a wooden leg. The straps was broke off of it, but barring that, it was a good enough leg, though it was too long for me and not long enough for Jim, and we couldn't find the other one, though we hunted all round.

And so, take it all round, we made a good haul.

This is the sort of list that a boy reader should pore over with delight; but the paragraph performs other functions of which the boy reader would be unaware. It provides the right counterpoise to the horror of the wrecked house and the corpse; it has a grim precision which tells the reader all he needs to know about the way of life of the human derelicts who had used the house; and (especially the wooden leg, and the fruitless search for its mate) reminds us at the right moment of the kinship of mind and the sympathy between the boy outcast from society and the negro fugitive from the injustice of society.

Huck in fact would be incomplete without Jim, who is almost as notable a creation as Huck himself. Huck is the passive observer of men and events, Jim the submissive sufferer from them; and they are equal in dignity. There is no passage in which their relationship is brought out more clearly than the conclusion of the chapter in which, after the two have become separated in the fog, Huck in the canoe and Jim on the raft, Huck, in his impulse of boyish mischief, persuades Jim for a time that the latter had dreamt the whole episode.

'. . . my heart wuz mos' broke bekase you wuz los', en I didn' k'yer no mo' what become er me en de raf'. En when I wake up en fine you back agin', all safe en soun', de tears come en I could a got down on my knees en kiss' yo' foot, I's so thankful. En all you wuz thinkin' 'bout wuz how you could make a fool uv ole Jim wid a lie. Dat truck dah is *trash*; en trash is what people is dat puts dirt on de head er dey fren's en makes 'em ashamed.' . . .

It was fifteen minutes before I could work myself up to go and humble myself to a nigger—but I done it, and I warn't ever sorry for it afterwards, neither.

This passage has been quoted before; and if I quote it again, it is because I wish to elicit from it one meaning that is, I think, usually overlooked. What is obvious in it is the pathos and dignity of Jim, and this is moving enough; but what I find still more disturbing, and still more unusual in literature, is the pathos and dignity of the boy, when reminded so humbly and humiliatingly, that his position in the world is not that of other boys, entitled from time to time to a practical joke; but that he must bear, and bear alone, the responsibility of a man.

It is Huck who gives the book style. The River gives the book its form. But for the River, the book might be only a sequence of adventures with a happy ending. A river, a very big and powerful river, is the only natural force that can wholly determine the course of human peregrination. At sea, the wanderer may sail or be carried by winds and currents in one direction or another; a change of wind or tide may determine fortune. In the prairie, the direction of movement is more or less at the choice of the caravan; among mountains there will often be an alternative, a guess at the most likely pass. But the river with its strong, swift current is the dictator to the raft or to the steamboat. It is a treacherous and capricious dictator. At one season, it may move sluggishly in a channel so narrow that, encountering it for the first time at that point, one can hardly believe that it has travelled already for hundreds of miles, and has yet many hundreds of miles to go; at another season, it may obliterate the low Illinois shore to a horizon of water, while in its bed it runs with a speed such that no man or beast can survive in it. At such times, it carries down human bodies, cattle and houses. At least twice, at St. Louis, the western and the eastern shores have been separated by the fall of bridges, until the designer of the great Eads Bridge devised a structure which could resist the floods. In my own childhood, it was not unusual for the spring freshet to interrupt railway travel; and then the traveller to the East had to take steamboat from the levee up to Alton, at a higher level on the Illinois shore, before he could begin his rail journey. The river is never wholly chartable; it changes its pace, it shifts its channel, unaccountably; it may suddenly efface a sandbar, and throw up another bar where before was navigable water.

It is the River that controls the voyage of Huck and Jim; that will not let them land at Cairo, where Jim could have reached freedom; it is the River that separates them and deposits Huck for a time in the Grangerford household; the River that re-unites them, and then compels upon them the unwelcome company of the King and the Duke. Recurrently we are reminded of its presence and its power.

> When I woke up, I didn't know where I was for a minute. I set up and looked around, a little scared. Then I remembered. The river looked miles and miles across. The moon was so bright I could a counted the drift-logs that went a-slipping along, black and still, hundreds of yards out from shore. Everything was dead quiet, and

it looked late, and *smelt* late. You know what I mean—I don't know the words to put it in. . . .

It was kind of solemn, drifting down the big still river, laying on our backs looking up at the stars, and we didn't ever feel like talking loud, and it warn't often that we laughed, only a little kind of a low chuckle. We had mighty good weather as a general thing, and nothing ever happened to us at all, that night, nor the next, nor the next.

Every night we passed towns, some of them away up on black hillsides, nothing but just a shiny bed of lights, not a house could you see. The fifth night we passed St. Louis, and it was like the whole world lit up. In St. Petersburg they used to say there was twenty or thirty thousand people in St. Louis, but I never believed it till I see that wonderful spread of lights at two o'clock that still night. There warn't a sound there; everybody was asleep.

We come to understand the River by seeing it through the eyes of the Boy; but the Boy is also the spirit of the River. *Huckleberry Finn*, like other great works of imagination, can give to every reader whatever he is capable of taking from it. On the most superficial level of observation, Huck is convincing as a boy. On the same level, the picture of social life on the shores of the Mississippi a hundred years ago is, I feel sure, accurate. On any level, Mark Twain makes you see the River, as it is and was and always will be, more clearly than the author of any other description of a river known to me. But you do not merely see the River, you do not merely become acquainted with it through the senses: you experience the River. Mark Twain, in his later years of success and fame, referred to his early life as a steamboat pilot as the happiest he had known. With all allowance for the illusions of age, we can agree that those years were the years in which he was most fully alive. Certainly, but for his having practised that calling, earned his living by that profession, he would never have gained the understanding which his genius for expression communicates in this book. In the pilot's daily struggle with the River, in the satisfaction of activity, in the constant attention to the River's unpredictable vagaries, his consciousness was fully occupied, and he absorbed knowledge of which, as an artist, he later made use. There are, perhaps, only two ways in which a writer can acquire the understanding of environment which he can later turn to account: by having spent his childhood in that environment—that is, living in it at a period of life in which one experiences much more than one is aware of; and by having had to struggle for a livelihood in that environment—a livelihood bearing no direct relation to any intention of writing about it, of *using* it as literary material. Most of Joseph Conrad's understanding came to him in the latter way. Mark Twain knew the Mississippi in both ways: he had spent his childhood on its banks, and he had earned his living matching his wits against its currents.

Thus the River makes the book a great book. As with Conrad, we are continually reminded of the power and terror of Nature, and the isolation and feebleness of Man. Conrad remains always the European observer of the tropics, the white man's eye contemplating the Congo and its black gods. But Mark Twain is a native, and the River God is his God. It is as a native that he accepts the River God, and it is the subjection of Man that gives to Man his dignity. For without some kind of God, Man is not even very interesting.

Readers sometimes deplore the fact that the story descends to the level of *Tom Sawyer* from the moment that Tom himself re-appears. Such readers protest that the escapades invented by Tom, in the attempted "rescue" of Jim, are only a tedious development of themes with which we were already too familiar—even while admitting that the escapades themselves are very amusing, and some of the incidental observations memorable.[1] But it is right that the mood of the end of the book should bring us back to that of the beginning. Or, if this was not the right ending for the book, what ending would have been right?

In *Huckleberry Finn* Mark Twain wrote a much greater book than he could have known he was writing. Perhaps all great works of art mean much more than the author could have been aware of meaning: certainly, *Huckleberry Finn* is the one book of Mark Twain's which, as a whole, has this unconsciousness. So what seems to be the rightness, of reverting at the end of the book to the mood of *Tom Sawyer,* was perhaps unconscious art. For Huckleberry Finn, neither a tragic nor a happy ending would be suitable. No worldly success or social satisfaction, no domestic consummation would be worthy of him; a tragic end also would reduce him to the level of those whom we pity. Huck Finn must come from nowhere and be bound for nowhere. His is not the independence of the typical or symbolic American Pioneer, but the independence of the vagabond. His existence questions the values of America as much as the values of Europe; he is as much an affront to the "pioneer spirit" as he is to "business enterprise"; he is in a state of nature as detached as the state of the saint. In a busy world, he represents the loafer; in an acquisitive and competitive world, he insists on living from hand to mouth. He could not be exhibited in any amorous encounters or engagements, in any of the juvenile affections which are appropriate to Tom Sawyer. He belongs neither to the Sunday School nor to the Reformatory. He has no beginning and no end. Hence, he can only disappear; and his disappearance can only be accomplished by bringing forward another performer to obscure the disappearance in a cloud of whimsicalities.

---

1. *e.g.* "*Jim* don't know anybody in China."

Like Huckleberry Finn, the River itself has no beginning or end. In its beginning, it is not yet the River; in its end, it is no longer the River. What we call its headwaters is only a selection from among the innumerable sources which flow together to compose it. At what point in its course does the Mississippi become what the Mississippi *means?* It is both one and many; it is the Mississippi of this book only after its union with the Big Muddy—the Missouri; it derives some of its character from the Ohio, the Tennessee and other confluents. And at the end it merely disappears among its deltas: it is no longer there, but it is still where it was, hundreds of miles to the North. The River cannot tolerate any design, to a story which is its story, that might interfere with its dominance. Things must merely happen, here and there, to the people who live along its shores or who commit themselves to its current. And it is as impossible for Huck as for the River to have a beginning or end—a career. So the book has the right, the only possible concluding sentence. I do not think that any book ever written ends more certainly with the right words:

But I reckon I got to light out for the Territory ahead of the rest, because Aunt Sally she's going to adopt me and civilize me, and I can't stand it. I been there before.

From *Huckleberry Finn* (New York: Chanticleer, 1950), pp. vii-xvi.

MARTIN STAPLES SHOCKLEY

The Structure of *Huckleberry Finn*

CONVENTIONAL COMMENT on *Huckleberry Finn* informs us that the novel is without structure. Professor George Feinstein tells us that "Clemens' conception of story form departs sharply from the views sanctified by critical tradition. He opposes a studied perfection of plot, favors instead a loose, spontaneous development of narrative."[1] In proclaiming *Huck* "the crown of our literature," Mr. Herman Wouk concedes this royal diadem to be a novel of shreds and patches, "a jerky, uneven, patchwork tale, as jerrybuilt as a pioneer's hut on the prairies, or a real estate development on Long Island. By the classic standards of European fiction it is one long barbarous mistake.[2]

Critics commonly classify *Huckleberry Finn* as a picaresque novel, the road being the river, little Huck the picaro, the novel consisting of a rambling series of amusing adventures. Professor Lionel Trilling stated this theory:

> The form of the book is based on the simplest of all novel-forms, the so-called picaresque novel, or novel of the road, which strings its incidents on the line of the hero's travels. But, as Pascal says, "Rivers are roads that move," and the movement of the road in its own mysterious life transmutes the primitive simplicity of the form: the road itself is the greatest character in this novel of the road, and the hero's departures from the river and his returns to it form a subtle and significant pattern. The linear simplicity of the picaresque novel is further modified by the story's having a clear dramatic organization; it has a beginning, a middle, and an end, and a mounting suspense of interest.[3]

Mr. Eliot joined Professor Trilling in attempting to justify the Phelps farm section as conclusion:

> Readers sometimes deplore the fact that the story descends to the level of *Tom Sawyer* from the moment that Tom himself reappears. Such readers protest that the escapades invented by Tom, in the attempted "rescue" of Jim, are only a tedious development of themes with which we were already too familiar—even while admitting that the escapades themselves are very amusing, and

some of the incidental observations memorable. But it is right that the mood of the end of book should bring us back to that of the beginning. Or, if this was not the right ending for the book, what ending would have been right? [4]

Disagreeing with both Trilling and Eliot, I consider this the wrong ending for the book; I propose another ending which I consider the right one.

Replying to the Trilling-Eliot interpretation, which defends the Phelps section, Professor Leo Marx writes:

> Such structural unity as Trilling and Eliot find is imposed upon the novel, and therefore is meretricious. It is a jerry-built structure, achieved only by the sacrifice of characters and theme. Here the controlling principle of form apparently is unity, but unfortunately a unity much too superficially conceived. [5]

Professor James M. Cox finds the structure determined by the juxtaposition and interplay of sets of symbols: civilization and the frontier, gentility and barbarism, freedom and bondage. [6] Professor Gilbert M. Rubenstein finds a "moral structure" built upon the major theme of human cruelty which "is central to every aspect of the plot and characterization." [7] Professor Frank Baldanza attempts to show that "without advanced planning, and spurred by momentary impulses, Mark Twain— in all probability unconsciously—constructed whole passages of *Huckleberry Finn* on the aesthetic principle of repetition and variation." [8]

In *Mark Twain As a Literary Artist*, Professor Gladys Bellamy devotes several pages to an analysis of *Huck*. She writes:

> In spite of its episodic nature, the book falls naturally into three thematic units. In the first sixteen chapters the theme has to do with what is of and from St. Petersburg: Huck, Tom, Nigger Jim and Pap. The second thematic unit includes the most strongly satiric, the most powerful part of the book, bringing Huck and Jim into contact with the outside world . . . The third thematic unit is short, a sort of coda to the rest, covering the period at the Phelps farm in which Tom reenters the story. This section repeats the romanticized motif of the first Part and thus brings the book around full-circle, before its close. [9]

Professor Bellamy then proceeds, following Professor Floyd Stovall, to interpret *Huckleberry Finn* as "a satire on institutionalism." [10]

The relationship of theme and structure is further considered by Professor Richard P. Adams, who says that "The basic structure, which expresses the theme of the boy's growth and which carries weight of

the incidents and the imagery throughout, is a pattern of symbolic
death and rebirth."[11] Like Bellamy, Adams finds a three-part structure:

> The beginning is Huck's life on shore in and around the village of
> St. Petersburg with the Widow Douglas and Pap. The middle, initi-
> ated by Huck's fake death, is his withdrawal from the life of soci-
> ety and civilization to the river; this withdrawal is repeated after
> each of his adventures on land. The end is his equivocal rebirth, his
> qualified return, under a false identity and with many reservations,
> to civilized life at the Phelps plantation.[12]

According to Professor Adams, Huck makes three major decisions:
1. to help Jim escape; 2. not to turn Jim in; 3. to go to hell to save Jim.
He concludes:

> The total result of these thematic, structural, and symbolic
> workings is a novel which has a remarkably high degree of consis-
> tency, coherence, and unity. Its theme is the growth of an individ-
> ual personality. Its crisis is the moral decision, repeated three
> times, to repudiate the conventions of society and to do the indi-
> vidually, humanly, right thing.[13]

Acknowledging my obligations to these critics and others, I propose
that *Huckleberry Finn* is thematically coherent and structurally unified.
I propose a logical, ordered, five-part structure, with introduction,
rising action, climax, falling action, conclusion, I propose proportion
and balance among these parts, achieving a total aesthetic harmony.

Part one, introduction, is set in the village. It provides the background of village life, introduces characters, establishes relationships,
creates the relaxed, leisurely mood which, flowing like the river, is
interrupted by effectively contrasting incidents of violence and horror.
Part one consists of six chapters.

Part two begins with chapter seven, in which Huck fools Pap and
gets away. The setting of part two is the raft and the river, with excursions ashore. Here the idyllic life of Huck and Jim on the raft contrasts
effectively with "civilized" life ashore, as incidents of fraud, greed,
cruelty, violence, culminating in the Grangerford-Shepherdson feud,
reveal the wickedness of "civilized" man. Part two consists of twelve
chapters, seven through eighteen.

Chapter nineteen begins a new sequence when the Duke and the
King come aboard. Part three differs from part two not only in the
introduction of two new characters; it is marked by a shift of emphasis:
there is less river and more land, hence the tone is less bucolic and more
satiric. The sequence of events in part three includes all those incidents

in which the Duke and the King participate, thirteen chapters, extending from chapter nineteen through chapter thirty-one.

Part four is set apart by another change in setting, character, and tone. Here is the Phelps farm, the coming of Tom Sawyer, and the burlesque rescue of Jim. Part four consists of eleven chapters, thirty-two through forty-two.

Part five is chapter forty-three, two short pages in which final dispositions are made and the last word is said.

This, I propose, divides the book logically, and achieves balance and proportion. The introduction is half as long as the three main parts, which are almost exactly equal, while the conclusion is properly brief.

But logic and proportion are not enough. Structure should clarify and emphasize theme. I propose to show the development of a consistent theme which inheres in the nature of the material, grows through the plot, reveals the development of the central character through struggle, provides minor climaxes which end each of the parts as effectively as a final curtain.

Huck introduces himself in the first sentence: "You don't know about me without you have read a book by the name of *The Adventures of Tom Sawyer;* but that ain't no matter." Four pages later, in the first paragraph of chapter two we meet "Miss Watson's big nigger, named Jim." Jim is characterized as simple, superstitious, credulous, as is Huck, who believes in Jim's hair-ball, "as big as your fist, which had been took out of the fourth stomach of an ox," as devotedly as does Jim.

The character of primary importance throughout the book is, of course, Huck. In each part, however, one character is of outstanding importance in relation to Huck. In part one it is Pap.

Huck is defined by his relationship to Pap, and this relationship motivates the action which begins part two, Huck's escape from Pap. I would point out the conclusion of part one, Pap's drunken monologue on government, and particularly the climactic and concluding paragraph of this monologue, because it is significant in relation to both structure and theme:

> Oh, yes, this is a wonderful government, wonderful. Why, looky here. There was a free nigger there from Ohio—a mullater, most as white as a white man. He had the whitest shirt on you ever see too, and the shiniest hat; and there ain't a man in that town that's got as fine clothes as what he had; and he had a gold watch and chain, and a silver-headed cane—the awfulest old gray-headed nabob in the state. And what do you think? They said he was a p'fessor in a college, and could talk all kinds of languages, and knowed everything. And that ain't the wust. They said he could vote when he was at home. Well that let me out. Thinks I, what is the country

a-coming to? It was 'lection day, and I was just about to go and vote myself if I warn't too drunk to get there; but when they told me there was a state in this country where they'd let that nigger vote, I drawed out. I says I'll never vote ag'in. Them's the very words I said: they all heard me: and the country may rot for all of me—I'll never vote ag'in as long as I live. And to see the cool way of that nigger—why he wouldn't 'a' give me the road if I hadn't shoved him out of the way. I says to the people, why ain't this nigger put up at auction and sold:—that's what I want to know. And what do you reckon they said? Why, they said he couldn't be sold till he'd been in the state six months and he hadn't been there that long yet. There, now—that's a specimen. They call that a govment that can't sell a free nigger till he's been in the state six months. Here's a govment that calls itself a govment, and lets on to be a govment, and thinks it is a govment, and yet's got to set stock-still for six whole months before it can take a-hold of a prowling, thieving, infernal, white-shirted, free nigger, and—

From these ideas, which are reported, not questioned by little Huck, the theme takes its beginning. The key phrase thrice repeated, is "free nigger."

Part two is the favorite of most readers and critics. Here the setting is the river, "the majestic, the magnificent Mississippi, rolling its mile-wide tide along, shining in the sun." The main characters are Huck and Jim, and the character of most importance in relation to Huck is Jim. There are several incidents; action rises from Huck's escape from Pap through the Grangerford-Shepherdson feud; and the curtain falls on Huck and Jim re-united on the raft.

Theme is developed through the relationship of Huck and Jim. In part two, as in part one, Jim enters in the second chapter. The note of superstition on which he enters, believing that Huck is a ghost, carries over the characterization and the relationship established in part one. This relationship is immediately developed through Huck's playing a trick on Jim, a trick in which Huck is responsible for Jim's being bitten by a rattlesnake. In this incident begins the working out of a new relationship between Huck and Jim. In the next chapter Huck discovers that Jim is in danger of being caught, and, without pausing to question motive, leads Jim in their escape. Afterwards Huck feels ashamed of himself for the mean trick he has played on the men who come to capture Jim. He says, "I played it as low down on them as I could."

Here begins the struggle, the complication of the plot, the development of character, the revelation of theme. Professor Edgar M. Branch states the theme as "the conflict between individual freedom and the restraints imposed by convention and force; or, within Huck's consciousness, the struggle between his intuitive morality and his conventional conscience".[14] After having stated the theme, Professor Branch concludes that "The degree of thematic form achieved in *Huckleberry Finn* is a rare accomplishment in Mark Twain's writing." Yet he upholds "the lack of rational narrative organization," and applauds the author for "denying the importance of formal structure."[15]

I suspect that Mark Twain, writing before Freud, might have identified "conscience" with "intuitive morality," rather than contrasting them as does Professor Branch. Mark, or Huck, uses "conscience" to mean "intuitive" morality as contrasted with "conventional" morality, or the expectations and demands of a society which Huck calls "civilized." It is his intuitive morality which demands that he acknowledge Jim's humanity, as opposed to the demand of "civilized" society that he turn Jim in as a runaway slave. This is the central struggle which I find clarified and emphasized through the "rational narrative organization" and "formal narrative structure" which Professor Branch fails to find.

The conflict, then, is between right and wrong. The theme is the individual's struggle to know and to do the right. Stated in other terms it is man's universal journey from innocence toward wisdom, or, if you prefer, the salvation of the human soul. Some people consider it the greatest of all themes.

The next Huck-versus-Jim episode is chapter fourteen, "Was Solomon wise?" This debate, a famous satire on formal logic, is far more. Jim's classic syllogism proving that a Frenchman is not a man is not the conclusion. The point, which is whether Jim is a man, is insinuated in Huck's last words, the end of the chapter: "I see it warn't no use wasting words—you can't learn a nigger to argue. So I quit."

Twain next adds the incident in which Huck deceives Jim, pretending to have been lost, and convincing Jim that it was all a dream. This is rising action; it intensifes Huck's moral struggle. Jim says:

> 'What do dey stan' for? I's gyne to tell you. When I got all wore out wid work, en wid de callin' for you, en went to sleep, my heart wuz mos' broke bekase you wuz los', en I didn't k'yer no mo' what become er me en de raf'. En when I wake up en find you back ag'in, all safe en soun', de tears come, en I could 'a' got down on my knees en kiss you foot, I's so thankful. En all you wuz thinking 'bout wuz how you could make a fool uv ole Jim wid a lie. Dat truck dah is *trash*; en trash is what people is dat puts dirt on de head er dey fren's en makes 'em ashamed.'
>
> Then he got up slow and walked to the wigwam, and went in there without saying anything but that. But that was enough. It made me feel so mean I could almost kissed *his* foot to get him to take it back.
>
> It was fifteen minutes before I could work myself up to go and

humble myself to a nigger; but I done it, and I warn't ever sorry for it afterward, neither.

This, of course, represents a victory for intuitive morality. Slowly and painfully Huck is coming to accept Jim's humanity, which Huck's —and Mark's—society could not accept. The conventional attitude is perhaps most succinctly stated by Huck himself in reply to Aunt Sally's query: "Anybody hurt?" "No'm. Killed a nigger," replies Huck, saying what he knows is expected of him by the kind, slave-owning, dear old lady.

Conventional criticism informs us that through Huck, Mark relives the happy days of his life on the river. I propose that through Huck, Mark relives the inner experience of an individual moral struggle against slavery. This, I propose, is the most profound and revealing remembrance.

The next chapter continues the struggle. Huck's conscience tells him that he is to blame for helping Jim to run off from his "rightful" owner:

> Conscience up and says . . . , "But you knowed he was running for his freedom and you could 'a' paddled ashore and told somebody." That was so—I couldn't get around that no way. That was where it pinched. Conscience says to me, "What had poor Miss Watson done to you that you could see her nigger go off right under your eyes and never say one single word? What did that poor old woman do to you that you could treat her so mean? Why, she tried to learn you your book, she tried to learn you your manners, she tried to be good to you every way she knowed how. That's what she done.

In other words, Miss Watson represents the demands of conventional society, of acquired mores as opposed to innate morality. The struggle is intensified when Huck hears Jim say:

> The first thing he would do when he got to a free state he would buy his wife, which was owned on a farm close to where Miss Watson lived; and then they would both work to buy the two children, and if their master wouldn't sell them they'd get an Ab'litionist to go and steal them.
> It most froze me to hear such talk . . . Here was this nigger, which I had as good as helped to run away, coming right out flatfooted and saying he would steal his children—children that belonged to a man I didn't even know, a man that hadn't ever done me no harm.

Following this, Huck says, "My conscience got to stirring me up hotter than ever until at last I says to it, 'Let up on me—it ain't too late yet—I'll paddle ashore at the first light and tell.' I felt easy and happy and light as a feather right off. All my troubles was gone."

Then comes the encounter with the two men who are searching for runaway niggers, and Huck devises the famous smallpox stratagem to save Jim. Assuring the men that "I won't let no runaway niggers get by me if I can help it," Huck returns to the raft.

> Feeling bad and low, because I knowed very well I had done wrong, and I see it warn't no use for me to try to do right; a body that don't get *started* right when he's little ain't got no show—when the pinch comes there ain't nothing to back him up and keep him to his work, and so he gets beat. Then I thought a minute, and says to myself, hold on; s'pose you'd 'a' done right and give Jim up, would you felt better than what you do now? No, says I, I'd feel bad—I'd feel just the same way I do now. Well, then, says I, what's the use you learning to do right when it's troublesome to do right and ain't no trouble to do wrong, and the wages is just the same? I was stuck. I couldn't answer that. So I rekoned I wouldn't bother no more about it, but after this always do whichever come handiest at the time.

This incident is the high point of the struggle in part two. It represents a significant development in Huck's understanding of his moral dilemma. In terms of literary art it prefigures the climax of the novel which comes in part three.

The next two chapters relate the Grangerford-Shepherdson feud. Then, at the end of chapter eighteen, act two gets a resounding curtain in the reunion of Huck and Jim. Huck's experiences with civilization are gradually clarifying for him the relationship of good and evil, evil being represented by the "proper" behaviour of the Grangerfords and the Shepherdsons, while in the words which conclude part two, "we said there warn't no home like a raft, after all. Other places seem so cramped and smothery, but a raft don't. You feel mighty free and easy and comfortable on a raft."

Part three brings aboard the Duke and the Dauphin, who together are the characters most important in relation to Huck through the thirteen chapters of this part. The setting is less on the river and more on the land, the cool and starry nights on the raft being replaced by the squalor and wretchedness of "civilized" life along the shore. We have assorted episodes of scoundrelism: the Royal Nonesuch, Boggs and Colonel Sherburn, the Wilks family. I would not claim that all these episodes relate directly to the issue of slavery. I would suggest, however, that all are related to the central theme, the moral struggle of the major character; that all present varied aspects of this moral struggle; that all contribute to little Huck's increasing moral awareness.

Jim is temporarily in the background; but we are kept aware of him and of Huck's dilemma. Between the Boggs and Wilks episode, chapter twenty-three reiterates the problem of Jim and his family. Huck's conclusion represents another step in his moral development. He says,

> I went to sleep, and Jim didn't even call me when it was my turn. He often done that. When I waked up just at daybreak he was sitting there with his head down betwixt his knees moaning and mourning to himself. I didn't take note nor let on. I knowed what it was about. He was thinking about his wife and children, away up yonder, and he was low and homesick; because he hadn't ever been away from home before in his life; and I do believe he cared as much for his people as white folks does for their'n. It don't seem natural, but I reckon it's so. He was often moaning and mourning that way nights, when he judged I was asleep, and saying, "Po' little 'Lizabeth' po' little Johnny! it's mighty hard; I spec' I ain't ever gwyne to see you no mo', no mo'!" He was a mighty good nigger, Jim was.

Then in chapter thirty-one, precisely at the end of part three, comes the climax prefigured in chapter sixteen. Entitled "You Can't Pray a Lie," this chapter presents Huck's great struggle and final decision, which is precipitated when the Duke and the King advertise Jim as a runaway slave in order to collect a reward for betraying him. Huck wrestles with his conscience, finally reaching the decision to do "right." His attempt to pray a lie dramatizes the struggle. In this climactic scene Huck is alone. He is, he says, "trying to make my mouth say I would do the right thing, and go and write to that nigger's owner and tell where he was; but deep down in me I knowed it was a lie, and He knowed it. You can't pray a lie—I found that out."

Huck writes to Miss Watson the letter which betrays Jim. At once, he "felt good and all washed clean of sin." Then immediately preceding the climax and preparing for it, Huck reviews his relationship with Jim, the trip down the river. Note the literary propriety, as well as the artistic effectiveness of this recapitulation at the point of crisis. Note also that this recapitulation serves to recall, as determining Huck's decision, precisely those episodes through which we have traced conflict and rising action. Then, pointing to and emphasizing the climactic sentence, one short paragraph says, in effect, "Look, this is it!" For, cementing theme and structure, here crisis (the irrevocable decision) and climax (the apex of rising action) coincide. Both occur in one terse statement:

> Jim before me all the time: in the day and in the night-time, sometimes moonlight, sometimes storms, and we a-floating along,

talking, and singing and laughing. But somehow I couldn't seem to strike no places to harden me against him but only the other kind. I'd see him how glad he was when I come back out of the fog; and when I come to him again in the swamp, up there where the feud was; and pet me, and do everything he could think of for me, and how good he always was; and at last I struck the time I saved him by telling the men we had smallpox aboard, and he was so grateful, and said I was the best friend old Jim ever had in the world, and the *only* one he's got now; and then I happened to look around and see that paper.

It was a close place. I took it up, and held it in my hand. I was a-trembling, because I'd got to decide, forever, betwixt two things, and I knowed it. I studied a minute, sort of holding my breath, and then says to myself:

"All right, then, I'll go to hell"—and tore it up.

At this point, the Pearly Gates swing wide, and the heavenly chorus swells. Mark Twain is saying: "Greater love hath no man," and "whoso would save his soul must lose it." Huck has won his moral struggle; innate goodness has triumphed over the internalized mores of Huck's civilization; through losing his soul, Huck has saved it. A tremendous curtain on Act III!

Part four, chapters thirty-two through forty-two, is again set off by change of setting, of characters, and of tone. Here the setting is the Phelps farm, and the character of greatest importance in relation to Huck is Tom Sawyer. Jim is no longer in the background, but comes again into the main action.

This, of course, is falling action. As such it lacks the interest and the intensity of the rising action of parts two and three. It may be, as critics have said, unnecessarily long; yet its eleven chapters balance with the twelve of part two and the thirteen of part three. There is a perceptible falling off, however, as there should be, a gradual release from anxiety as the reader is brought down from the climax and as the story is brought to its close.

The tone is less serious; satire is less strong; humor, absurdity, burlesque are developed. The moral crisis past, the characters relax. Huck has resolved his dilemma, and now his conscience is less troublesome. There is evidence of moral maturity in his last comment on the Duke and the King: "I was sorry for them poor pitiful rascals, and it seemed like I couldn't ever feel any hardness against them any more in the world. Human beings *can* be awful cruel to one another."

This Phelps farm section has caused most of the confusion among critics, who have consistently considered it the conclusion of the novel. Both Trilling and Eliot consider it the end, and attempt to justify it; Marx considers it the end, and exposes its weakness as a conclusion.

Others have attempted either to apologize for it or to account for it in various ingenious ways. It has been generally conceded to be a mistake, the inexcusable flaw, the greatest weakness of the novel, and has been generally cited as proof of Mark Twain's failure to achieve form.

It is important, therefore, to realize that the Phelps farm chapters constitute not conclusion but falling action. Hence the five-part structure, separating conclusion from falling action, is essential because it is the only structure which achieves this necessary separation.

Failure to perceive the importance of the final chapter as conclusion leads Professor Charles Kaplan into the mistake of thinking that the Phelps farm section shows "Twain's final acquiescence to the world which has been criticized throughout."[16] Twain (or Huck) does not acquiesce; he repudiates. Professor Kaplan is also, I think, in error when he says that "Huck, by the end of the novel, has been trapped."[17] Huck has not been trapped. He is free. He "lights out." The conclusion, therefore, is not weak, but strong because Huck is both physically and morally free.

Part five, conclusion, consists of two short pages titled "Chapter the Last: Nothing More to Write." Here final dispositions of characters are made; and here, significantly, Huck remains consistent. He has grown from innocence to wisdom; he has savored "civilized" society and rejected it: "I can't stand it," he says, "I been there before." Now, having repudiated the demands of that society, he is ready to live by innate morality, a free man. "So there ain't nothing more to write about."

From *The South-Central Bulletin,* 20 (Winter 1960), 3-10.

1. "Mark Twain's Idea of Story Structure" *American Literature,* XVIII (May, 1946), 160.

2. "The Voice of Huckleberry Finn," *The Sunday Denver Post,* August 5, 1956.

3. "Mark Twain, *The Adventures of Huckleberry Finn.* (New York, Rinehart & Co., 1948). Introduction, p. xvi. Quotations are from this edition.

4. T. S. Eliot, "Introduction," *The Adventures of Huckleberry Finn,* London, 1950, p. xv.

5. "Mr. Eliot, Mr. Trilling, and Huckleberry Finn," *American Scholar,* XXII (Autumn, 1953), 423-440.

6. "Remarks on the Sad Initiation of Huckleberry Finn," *Sewanee Review,* XLII (Summer, 1954), 389-405.

7. "The Moral Structure of Huckleberry Finn," *College English,* XVIII (November, 1956), 74.

8. "The Structure of Huckleberry Finn," *American Literature,* XVVII (November, 1955), 350.

9. Norman, University of Oklahoma Press, 1950, p. 338.

10. Ibid., p. 340.

11. "The Unity and Coherence of Huckleberry Finn," *Tulane Studies in English,* VI (1956), 89.

12. Ibid., p. 90.

13. Ibid., p. 103.

14. "The Two Providences: Thematic Form in Huckleberry Finn," *College English*, XI, (January, 1950), 188.

15. Ibid., p. 194.

16. "Holden and Huck: the Odysseys of Youth," *College English*, XVIII (November, 1956), 78.

17. Ibid.

HENRY NASH SMITH

A Sound Heart and a Deformed Conscience

IN WRITING *Huckleberry Finn* Mark Twain found a way to organize into a larger structure the insights that earlier humorists had recorded in their brief anecdotes. This technical accomplishment was of course inseparable from the process of discovering new meanings in his material. His development as a writer was a dialectic interplay in which the reach of his imagination imposed a constant strain on his technical resources, and innovations of method in turn opened up new vistas before his imagination.

The dialectic process is particularly striking in the gestation of *Huckleberry Finn*. The use of Huck as a narrative persona, with the consequent elimination of the author as an intruding presence in the story, resolved the difficulties about point of view and style that had been so conspicuous in the earlier books. But turning the story over to Huck brought into view previously unsuspected literary potentialities in the vernacular perspective, particularly the possibility of using vernacular speech for serious purposes and of transforming the vernacular narrator from a mere persona into a character with human depth. Mark Twain's response to the challenge made *Huckleberry Finn* the greatest of his books and one of the two or three acknowledged masterpieces of American literature. Yet this triumph created a new technical problem to which there was no solution; for what had begun as a comic story developed incipiently tragic implications contradicting the premises of comedy.

Huckleberry Finn thus contains three main elements. The most conspicuous is the story of Huck's and Jim's adventures in their flight toward freedom. Jim is running away from actual slavery, Huck from the cruelty of his father, from the well-intentioned "sivilizing" efforts of Miss Watson and the Widow Douglas, from respectability and routine in general. The second element in the novel is social satire of the towns along the river. The satire is often transcendently funny, especially in episodes involving the rascally Duke and King, but it can also deal in appalling violence, as in the Grangerford-Shepherdson feud or Colonel Sherburn's murder of the helpless Boggs. The third major element in the book is the developing characterization of Huck.

All three elements must have been present to Mark Twain's mind in some sense from the beginning, for much of the book's greatness lies in its basic coherence, the complex interrelation of its parts. Nevertheless, the intensive study devoted to it in recent years, particularly Walter Blair's establishment of the chronology of its composition, has demonstrated that Mark Twain's search for a structure capable of doing justice to his conceptions of theme and character passed through several stages. He did not see clearly where he was going when he began to write, and we can observe him in the act of making discoveries both in meaning and in method as he goes along.

The narrative tends to increase in depth as it moves from the adventure story of the early chapters into the social satire of the long middle section, and thence to the ultimate psychological penetration of Huck's character in the moral crisis of Chapter 31. Since the crisis is brought on by the shock of the definitive failure of Huck's effort to help Jim, it marks the real end of the quest for freedom. The perplexing final sequence on the Phelps plantation is best regarded as a maneuver by which Mark Twain beats his way back from incipient tragedy to the comic resolution called for by the original conception of the story. . . .

Huck is revolted by the King's hypocrisy: "I never seen anything so disgusting." He has had a similar reaction to the brutality of the feud: "It made me so sick I most fell out of the tree." In describing such scenes he speaks as moral man viewing an immoral society, an observer who is himself free of the vices and even the weaknesses he describes. Mark Twain's satiric method requires that Huck be a mask for the writer, not a fully developed character. The method has great ironic force, and is in itself a technical landmark in the history of American fiction, but it prevents Mark Twain from doing full justice to Huck as a person in his own right, capable of mistakes in perception and judgment, troubled by doubts and conflicting impulses.

Even in the chapters written during the original burst of composition in 1876 the character of Huck is shown to have depths and complexities not relevant to the immediate context. Huck's and Jim's journey down the river begins simply as a flight from physical danger; and the first episodes of the voyage have little bearing on the novelistic possibilities in the strange comradeship between outcast boy and escaped slave. But in Chapter 15, when Huck plays a prank on Jim by persuading him that the separation in the fog was only a dream, Jim's dignified and moving rebuke suddenly opens up a new dimension in the relation. Huck's humble apology is striking evidence of growth in moral insight. It leads naturally to the next chapter in which Mark Twain causes Huck to face up for the first time to the fact that he is helping a slave to escape. It is as if the writer himself were discovering unsuspected meanings in what he had thought of as a story of picaresque adventure. The incipient contradiction between narrative plan and increasing depth in Huck's character must have been as disconcerting to Mark Twain as the difficulty of finding a way to account for Huck's and Jim's continuing

southward past the mouth of the Ohio. It was doubtless the conver-
gence of the two problems that led him to put aside the manuscript
near the end of Chapter 16.

The introduction of the Duke and the King not only took care of
the awkwardness in the plot but also allowed Mark Twain to postpone
the exploration of Huck's moral dilemma. If Huck is not a free agent he
is not responsible for what happens and is spared the agonies of choice.
Throughout the long middle section, while he is primarily an observer,
he is free of inner conflict because he is endowed by implication with
Mark Twain's own unambiguous attitude toward the fraud and folly he
witnesses.

In Chapter 31, however, Huck escapes from his captors and faces
once again the responsibility for deciding on a course of action. His
situation is much more desperate than it had been at the time of his
first struggle with his conscience. The raft has borne Jim hundreds of
miles downstream from the pathway of escape and the King has turned
him over to Silas Phelps as a runaway slave. The quest for freedom has
"all come to nothing, everything all busted up and ruined." Huck
thinks of notifying Miss Watson where Jim is, since if he must be a slave
he would be better off "at home where his family was." But then Huck
realizes that Miss Watson would probably sell Jim down the river as a
punishment for running away. Furthermore, Huck himself would be
denounced by everyone for his part in the affair. In this fashion his
mind comes back once again to the unparalleled wickedness of acting as
accomplice in a slave's escape.

The account of Huck's mental struggle in the next two or three
pages is the emotional climax of the story. It draws together the theme
of flight from bondage and the social satire of the middle section, for
Huck is trying to work himself clear of the perverted value system of
St. Petersburg. Both adventure story and satire, however, are now subordinate to an exploration of Huck's psyche which is the ultimate
achievement of the book. The issue is identical with that of the first
moral crisis, but the later passage is much more intense and richer in
implication. The differences appear clearly if the two crises are compared in detail.

In Chapter 16 Huck is startled into a realization of his predicament
when he hears Jim, on the lookout for Cairo at the mouth of the Ohio,
declare that "he'd be a free man the minute he seen it, but if he missed
it he'd be in a slave country again and no more show for freedom."
Huck says: "I begun to get it through my head that he *was* most
free—and who was to blame for it? Why, *me*. I couldn't get that out of
my conscience, no how nor no way." He dramatizes his inner debate by
quoting the words in which his conscience denounces him: "What had
poor Miss Watson done to you that you could see her nigger go off right
under your eyes and never say one single word? What did that poor old

woman do to you that you could treat her so mean? Why, she tried to
learn you your book, she tried to learn you your manners, she tried to
be good to you every way she knowed how. *That's* what she done."
The counterargument is provided by Jim, who seems to guess what is
passing through Huck's mind and does what he can to invoke the force
of friendship and gratitude: "Pooty soon I'll be a-shout'n' for joy, en
I'll say, it's all on accounts o' Huck; I's a free man, en I couldn't ever
ben free ef it hadn' ben for Huck: Huck done it. Jim won't ever forgit
you, Huck; you's de bes' fren' Jim's ever had; en you's de *only* fren' ole
Jim's got now." Huck nevertheless sets out for the shore in the canoe
"all in a sweat to tell on" Jim, but when he is intercepted by the two
slave hunters in a skiff he suddenly contrives a cunning device to ward
them off. We are given no details about how his inner conflict was
resolved.

In the later crisis Huck provides a much more circumstantial account
of what passes through his mind. He is now quite alone; the outcome of
the debate is not affected by any stimulus from the outside. It is the
memory of Jim's kindness and goodness rather than Jim's actual voice
that impels Huck to defy his conscience: "I see Jim before me all the
time: in the day and in the night-time, sometimes moonlight, sometimes storms, and we a-floating along, talking and singing and laughing." The most striking feature of this later crisis is the fact that Huck's
conscience, which formerly had employed only secular arguments, now
deals heavily in religious cant:

> At last, when it hit me all of a sudden that here was the plain hand
> of Providence slapping me in the face and letting me know my
> wickedness was being watched all the time from up there in
> heaven, whilst I was stealing a poor old woman's nigger that hadn't
> ever done me no harm, and now was showing me there's One that's
> always on the lookout, and ain't a-going to allow no such miserable
> doings to go only just so fur and no further, I most dropped in my
> tracks I was so scared.

In the earlier debate the voice of Huck's conscience is quoted directly, but the bulk of the later exhortation is reported in indirect discourse. This apparently simple change in method has remarkable consequences. According to the conventions of first-person narrative, the
narrator functions as a neutral medium in reporting dialogue. He remembers the speeches to other characters but they pass through his
mind without affecting him. When Huck's conscience speaks within
quotation marks it is in effect a character in the story, and he is not
responsible for what it says. But when he paraphrases the admonitions
of his conscience they are incorporated into his own discourse. Thus
although Huck is obviously remembering the bits of theological jargon

from sermons justifying slavery, they have become a part of his vocabulary.

The device of having Huck paraphrase rather than quote the voice of conscience may have been suggested to Mark Twain by a discovery he made in revising Huck's report of the King's address to the mourners in the Wilks parlor (Chapter 25). The manuscript version of the passage shows that the King's remarks were composed as a direct quotation, but in the published text they have been put, with a minimum of verbal change, into indirect discourse. The removal of the barrier of quotation marks brings Huck into much more intimate contact with the King's "rot and slush" despite the fact that the paraphrase quivers with disapproval. The voice of conscience speaks in the precise accents of the King but Huck is now completely uncritical. He does not question its moral authority; it is morality personified. The greater subtlety of the later passage illustrates the difference between the necessarily shallow characterization of Huck while he was being used merely as a narrative persona, and the profound insight which Mark Twain eventually brought to bear on his protagonist.

The recognition of complexity in Huck's character enabled Mark Twain to do full justice to the conflict between vernacular values and the dominant culture. By situating in a single consciousness both the perverted moral code of a society on slavery and the vernacular commitment to freedom and spontaneity, he was able to represent the opposed perspectives as alternative modes of experience for the same character. In this way he gets rid of the confusions surrounding the pronoun "I" in the earlier books, where it sometimes designates the author speaking in his own person, sometimes an entirely distinct fictional character. Furthermore, the insight that enabled him to recognize the conflict between accepted values and vernacular protest as a struggle within a single mind does justice to its moral depth, whereas the device he had used earlier—in *The Innocents Abroad*, for example—of identifying the two perspectives with separate characters had flattened the issue out into melodrama. The satire of a decadent slaveholding society gains immensely in force when Mark Twain demonstrates that even the outcast Huck has been in part perverted by it. Huck's conscience is simply the attitudes he has taken over from his environment. What is still sound in him is an impulse from the deepest level of his personality that struggles against the overlay of prejudice and false valuation imposed on all members of the society in the name of religion, morality, law, and refinement. . . .

From *Mark Twain: The Development of a Writer* (Cambridge: Belknap Press of Harvard Univ. Press, 1962), pp. 113-14, 118-22.

WILLIAM B. DILLINGHAM

Setting and Theme in *Tom Sawyer*

IN RECENT YEARS *The Adventures of Tom Sawyer* has quietly gained a secure position in American literature as a coherent work of art. Those who think of the book chiefly as an unordered collection of Twain's boyhood reminiscences[1] have been effectively answered by a host of critics beginning with Walter Blair in his article "On the Structure of *Tom Sawyer.*"[2] Blair persuasively argued that the novel concerns itself with Tom's maturation and pointed to the following four episodes which serve as the crucial tests in this process of growing up: Tom's romance with Becky, the Muff Potter incident, the Jackson's Island episode, and the Injun Joe story. These incidents, according to Blair, encompass the action of all but four of the thirty-five chapters of the novel. At the beginning of each episode Tom engages in a childish adventure, but by the end of that section he acts more maturely. His maturing accomplishment in each instance is applauded by the adults of St. Petersburg. As the novel ends, Tom is no longer the childish youth of the first part of the book; he is now on the threshold of the adult world. This analysis of the theme and structure of Tom Sawyer has been accepted by most recent critics of the novel.[3]

The work of Blair, Lewis Leary and others has convincingly revealed that *Tom Sawyer* has organization and purpose worthy of serious scholarly attention. The validity of this conclusion is even more apparent after an examination of the part setting plays in enhancing the theme of Tom's maturation.[4]

The principal tensions in Tom's growth are those between freedom and involvement, illusion and reality. Each of these influences is represented by one of the four settings of the story. For Tom and his fellows, Jackson's Island is the symbol of escape, of freedom from the troubles and responsibilities of homelife. St. Petersburg, on the other hand, stands in opposition to the isolated island as the symbol of involvement. The world of childish illusion, the dream world of youth, is embodied in Cardiff Hill, and the cave is that land opposed to the hill, the place of dark reality.

Early in the book Tom lives in the village, dreaming of adventure and escape from responsibility. He exists in the village, but he neither understands nor accepts its values. The prime value of the village, "respectability," has no place in Tom's juvenile thought. He admires Huck Finn for his lack of respectability, wishing that he could himself throw off the garments of civilization and live as does Huck. He intensely dislikes his respectable half brother Sid and abhors the village's "model boy." At this stage Tom has not identified himself with the village. His world is that of childhood innocence, illusion.

Chapter II begins with the symbol of this dream world, Cardiff Hill. In a lyrical description filled with such words as "morning," "summer," "bright," "fresh," "young," "spring," "bloom," and "blossoms," Twain first pictures Cardiff Hill in the background of St. Petersburg: "Cardiff Hill, beyond the village and above it, was green with vegetation, and it lay just far enough away to seem a Delectable Land, dreamy, reposeful, and inviting" (p. 12).[5] In a symbolic sense Cardiff Hill is always "beyond" and "above" the world of the village. When Tom yearns to escape from the drudgery of school, he views the Delectable Land of Cardiff Hill with longing: "Away off in the flaming sunshine, Cardiff Hill lifted its soft green sides through a shimmering veil of heat, tinted with the purple of distance. . . . Tom's heart ached to be free. . . ." (p. 65). Here again the hill is described in terms of light and color. Later, Tom in one of his adolescent fits of anger, runs away from Becky to his Delectable Land. From there, the schoolhouse below seemed "hardly distinguishable" (p. 73). On or near this same setting Tom plays Robin Hood in his dream world and with Huck Finn searches for illusory gold. Significantly, however, he finds no actual gold there. His material wealth, which carries with it mature responsibilities, is found elsewhere—in the world of darker reality, the cave. Tom's imaginary or actual travels to Cardiff Hill are short-lived. Always he returns to the village and finally the Delectable Land disappears from his thoughts and from the book.

Tom is also escaping from the village when he goes to Jackson's Island with Joe Harper and Huck. Unlike Cardiff Hill, however, the island is never described in terms of dream and illusion. It stands for the actual possibility of freedom whereas the hill is only the dream. Like Cardiff Hill, however, Jackson's Island contrasts sharply with the village. Three miles below St. Petersburg, "it was not inhabited: it lay far over toward the further shore, abreast a dense and almost wholly unpeopled forest" (p. 112). For a while the boys are successful in their search for freedom. "It's just the life for me," Tom remarks. "You don't have to get up, mornings, and you don't have to go to school, and wash, and all that blame foolishness" (p. 117). Loneliness, however, soon forces Tom to give up the isolation of freedom and return again to the village. As Blair has pointed out, this episode begins with Tom's childish running away from responsibility and mature conduct and ends with an act indicative of growth: his concern for Aunt Polly's feelings.

He has taken a major step away from the careless freedom of youth toward adult involvement.

Tom's last journey from the village is unlike his escapes to Cardiff Hill and Jackson's Island. Tom, Becky and the youths of St. Petersburg go to the great cave on an excursion. This time Tom is not running away to be free; he is a part of a larger social group, which is making a trip sanctioned by the grownups of St. Petersburg. Furthermore, Huck Finn is not with Tom this time. Huck is, as Lewis Leary has shown, the unchanging representative of innocence and freedom in the book. Unlike Tom and his friends on the party, Huck is never to accept the values of maturity. It is thus appropriate that Tom is without Huck's company in the ordeal of the cave, an experience which leads to Tom's final growth in the story.

The cave in every way is the antithesis of the hill. Here Tom does not dream the dreams of childhood. In the cave he is introduced to the terrors of fear and death. For the first time on one of his excursions from the village he is no longer playing; he is compelled to face reality as he never has before. In contrast to the hill, the cave is described not in words suggesting light and color but in terms of darkness and tangled complexity. It is a place of "deep gloom," an "intricate tangle of rifts and chasms" (p. 232). Whereas Cardiff Hill is associated with youth, the cave is shown as timeless, ageless. The drop of water which Injun Joe catches to drink was

> falling when the Pyramids were new; when Troy fell; when the foundations of Rome were laid; when Christ was crucified; when the Conqueror created the British empire; when Columbus sailed; when the massacre at Lexington was "news." It is falling now; it will still be falling when all these things shall have sunk down the afternoon of history and the twilight of tradition and been swallowed up in the thick night of oblivion (pp. 268-269).

When Tom and Becky become separated from their friends and lose their way in the complicated maze of the cave, they face starvation or a terrible fall into one of the endless chasms and death. Tom comforts Becky, with mature foresight rations his meager food, and only when absolutely necessary tells Becky of the seriousness of their plight. He reveals an even greater understanding of others' feelings than he exhibited at the end of the Jackson's Island episode. When he and the villagers find the body of Injun Joe at the mouth of the cave, a more adult Tom Sawyer, matured by suffering, feels pity for him. "Tom was touched, for he knew by his own experience how this wretch had suffered" (p. 267).

The cave, then, is the world of darker reality for Tom. If Cardiff Hill is the symbol of carefree childish illusion, the cave suggests the stark, unpleasant, and inexplicable realities of life. Only through his intimate and terrible introduction to these realities can Tom become a member of the mature world of the village. He has known fear before and he has witnessed death, but only in the cave do they become personal truths for him. Although Tom is not actually "reborn" in the cave, he does undergo an initiation which is represented symbolically. Tom and Becky spend three days and three nights in the eternal night of the cave, and then, near the sign of the cross at Injun Joe's lair, Tom finds his way out of the darkness into the light and the vision of the vital Mississippi flowing by. The powerful impact of Tom's emergence into the open from the cave has seldom been pointed out in studies of the book. In context, this description of Tom's groping toward the light is profoundly moving. Without real hope he leaves Becky behind and using his kite line explores various avenues of the cave. "He followed two avenues as far as his kite-line would reach; . . . he followed a third to the fullest stretch of the kite-line, and was about to turn back when he glimpsed a far off speck that looked like daylight; dropped the line and groped toward it, pushed his head and shoulders through a small hole and saw the broad Mississippi rolling by!" (p. 264).

Tom's "salvation" and new growth, even though represented in terms quite suggestive of Christian rebirth, are in Twain's view no cause for jubilation. Tom's emergence from three days and nights in the cave brings him closer than ever before to the values of the village, and for Twain the loss of childhood illusion is always sad. In the course of the novel, Tom never takes the final step across the shadow-line to adulthood. He can still organize a gang of "robbers" at the end. The book's tone, therefore, never approaches the bitterness of Twain's more pessimistic work. Nevertheless, it is evident that Tom has, as Walter Blair says, "gone over to the side of the enemy";[6] his "salvation" into the society of the village is rather sadly ironic.

Two of Tom's final conversations with Huck point up his change. When Tom and Huck approach the Widow Douglas's house near the end, and discover a large group of the citizens of St. Petersburg waiting for them, Huck wants to leave, but Tom no longer wants to escape the adult world. "It ain't anything," he tells Huck. "I don't mind it a bit. I'll take care of you" (p. 281). Later Huck, who still has not accepted the way of adults, escapes the Widow's care, but Tom seeks him out, tells him "the trouble he had been causing," and urges him to go back (p. 287). When Huck complains of his loss of freedom in the systematized world of civilization, Tom's answer is "Well, everybody does that way, Huck" (p. 288). And he pleads with Huck to "try this thing just awhile longer," assuring him that he will come to like it. Tom quickly sees, however, that he must apply greater pressure, and he tells Huck, "We can't let you into the gang if you ain't respectable, you know" (p. 290). The Tom Sawyer of the whitewashing episode who abhorred "respectability," the principal value of the village, thus comes to accept it. He tells Huck that he does not wish to exclude him from the gang, but if he is not respectable, "what would people say?" (p. 290). With this dialogue between Tom and Huck the novel closes.

In *Tom Sawyer*, therefore, setting is suggestive of the conflicting influences in Tom's maturation. The foreground of the story is the village, representative of involvement. Here is Tom's family, the church (and the graveyard), the neighbors, and the school. In the course of the novel Tom tries several times to escape the village and its values, but he ends by accepting it in large measure. Jackson's Island suggests the opposite of the village, that is, complete, if immature, individual freedom. Tom attempts to be rid of the shackles of the adult realm of St. Petersburg when he runs away to Jackson's Island. He finds involvement inevitable, however, and returns. The tension of appearance and reality in Tom's growth is seen in the opposition of Cardiff Hill and the cave. Cardiff Hill is Tom's "Delectable Land," his childhood dream world which he must leave behind. The cave is symbolic of the stark realities of life, unpleasant but ageless. For Tom the experience in the cave is his final trial, and he returns for the last time to the village on the brink of adulthood.

From *Mark Twain Journal,* 12 (Spring 1964), 6-8.

1. See, for example, DeLancey Ferguson, *Mark Twain: Man and Legend* (Indianapolis, 1943), p. 176; Alexander Cowie, *The Rise of the American Novel* (New York, 1948), p. 609; and Roger Asselineau, *The Literary Reputation of Mark Twain from 1910 to 1950* (Paris, 1954), p. 58.

2. *Modern Philology,* XXXVII (August, 1939), 75-88.

3. See Gladys Bellamy, *Mark Twain as a Literary Artist* (Norman, 1950), pp. 334-335; Dixon Wecter, "Mark Twain," *Literary History of the United States,* ed. Robert E. Spiller, et al. (New York, 1953), p. 930; Lewis Leary, "Tom, Huck: Innocence on Trial," *Virginia Quarterly Review,* XXX (Summer, 1954), 417-430; and Hamlin L. Hill, "The Composition and the Structure of *Tom Sawyer*," *American Literature,* XXXII (January, 1961), 379-392.

4. In his article "*Tom Sawyer* and the Use of Novels," *American Quarterly,* IX (Summer, 1957), 209-216, Louis D. Rubin has effectively indicated the value of one of the four settings, Cardiff Hill, in relation to theme.

5. Harper's Modern Classics (New York, 1950). All page references are to this edition.

6. Blair, p. 88.

JUDITH FETTERLEY

The Sanctioned Rebel

ONE OF THE major rhythms of *The Adventures of Tom Sawyer* is established in its opening lines: " 'Tom!' No answer. 'Tom!' No answer. 'What's gone with that boy, I wonder? You, TOM!' "[1] Much of the action of the novel is a variation on this theme of looking for Tom, for in the world of St. Petersburg the boy, Tom, is central. It is he who creates the major occasions for the town, and the emotional arcs of the book are described by his being lost or found. When Tom is thought lost, the town is in dismay; when he is found, it rejoices:

> The alarm swept from lip to lip, from group to group, from street to street, and within five minutes the bells were wildly clanging and the whole town was up! The Cardiff Hill episode sank into instant insignificance, the burglars were forgotten, horses were saddled, skiffs were manned, the ferryboat ordered out, and before the horror was half an hour old two hundred men were pouring down highroad and river toward the cave (p. 248). . . .
> Away in the middle of the night a wild peal burst from the village bells and in a moment the streets were swarming with frantic half-clad people, who shouted, "Turn out! turn out! they're found! they're found!" Tin pans and horns were added to the din, the population massed itself and moved toward the river, met the children coming in an open carriage drawn by shouting citizens, thronged around it, joined its homeward march, and swept magnificently up the main street roaring huzzah after huzzah! (pp. 263-64).

The world of St. Petersburg is dull and sleepy, and its arch enemy is the boredom which lies at its heart, making it so sensation-hungry that everything that happens is greeted as an entertainment. Thus the discovery of Dr. Robinson's murder constitutes a local holiday for which school is dismissed. Thus the town turns out to fill the church as never before for the spectacle of a triple funeral. Thus the trial of Muff Potter is the biggest entertainment of the summer; and when Tom finally decides to testify at the trial, he does so as much out of a sense of what is dramatically appropriate and will improve the show as he does out of a tormented conscience.

The boredom which lies at the heart of St. Petersburg is most fully pictured in the scenes which take place in the Sunday school and church the first Sunday of the novel. The dreadful monotony of Sunday school text, or prayer and sermon, the painful rigidity of never-varying rituals, symbolized by the superintendent's clothes—"a fence that compelled a straight lookout ahead, and a turning of the whole body when a side view was required" (p. 35)—is relieved only by a few paper wads, an occasional scuffle, a fly to be caught. The world of St. Petersburg is trapped into boredom by its own hypocrisy, by its refusal to admit how dull and uninteresting the things which it professes to value really are. It is against this background that Tom's centrality to St. Petersburg can be understood. He provides life, interest, amusement; he is a master entertainer with a bug for every occasion. No wonder St. Petersburg is always looking for Tom.

One of the central scenes which defines this aspect of the interrelation of Tom and his society is the moment in church when Tom discovers and releases his pinch bug. Tom's boredom has reached painful proportions; the momentary flicker of interest aroused by the image of the little child leading the lion and lamb before the hosts at Judgment Day has faded. Then he remembers his pinch bug, a "treasure" of the first order. He takes it out, it bites him, and he flips it on the floor. Immediately the congregation stirs itself; at last something is happening. A few minutes later a poodle which is the very image of the congregation, bored and sleepy, comes along and, like the congregation, begins to take an interest in the bug and to play with it. But after awhile he forgets about the bug and in starting to go to sleep, sits on it, whereupon it promptly bites him and sends him tearing around the church and ultimately out a window. "Tom Sawyer went home quite cheerful, thinking to himself that there was some satisfaction about divine service when there was a bit of variety in it" (p. 49). He has provided a brilliant entertainment and won the thanks of the congregation, for his act has not only amused them but has made it impossible for church to continue.

The other center of boredom in this world is school, and once again Tom has a bug to relieve him. Tom is bored to a point almost beyond endurance when he sticks his hand in his pocket and discovers the tick he has just purchased from Huck Finn: "his face lit up with a glow of gratitude that was prayer" (p. 65). His comrade, Joe Harper, as painfully bored as Tom, greets the tick and its promise of pleasure "deeply and gratefully" (p. 66). The language which describes the discovery of the tick is an impressive index of the boredom of school. But again the boys are not the only ones bored. The schoolmaster, Mr. Dobbins, is asleep when Tom comes in and only wakes up long enough to switch him. Tom's tick and his play with it become equally the source of the schoolmaster's interest: "He had contemplated a good part of the performance before he contributed his bit of variety to it" (p. 67). The switching is part of the complex game which the boys and adults play in order to make school bearable. It is the mode by which the teacher is allowed to save face and keep on professing his interest in school. It in no way prevents Tom from continuing to create interest through his pranks, for, unlike the world of Dickens, the switching in Tom's world leaves neither psychological nor physical scars. It is, indeed, the mark of the boys' success in gaining attention and creating interest; it is a modest form of showing off for both boys and teacher. The relationship between the adults and children in this novel is deeply symbiotic.

Tom's interactions with Aunt Polly develop another dimension of this relationship. Aunt Polly, like the rest of St. Petersburg, loves Tom, because he makes her laugh and gives variety to her life. But Aunt Polly expresses her affection for Tom by constantly rapping him on the head with her thimble, setting traps to catch him in lies, carping at him for being bad and breaking her heart, and enforcing labor on his holidays. She never comes out and openly says what Tom means to her until she thinks he is dead. In part, Aunt Polly is a victim of her own hypocrisy and unreality. She refuses to take account of the split which she everywhere expresses between her heart and her conscience, with its conception of duty. Thus she is never free to say what she truly feels. But this is really a very small part of the psychology behind Aunt Polly's actions. Tom knows that Aunt Polly's thimble on his head, like Dobbins's switching, is an index of the place he holds in her heart; thus he worries only when she does not rap him. But much more important, Tom knows that it is her resistance, her posture of disapproval, which creates his pleasure.

The fact that the boys' world of pranks is no fun without the existence of an adult world to prohibit them is made clear in a number of scenes in the story. When school is finally over and vacation finally comes, there is nothing Tom wants to do. What has happened to the lure of Cardiff Hill, which called to him so irresistibly through the schoolroom window? Clearly "hooky" is one thing and vacation another. When the boys run off to Jackson's Island everything is bully for the first day or so, but pretty soon they lose interest in going naked and sleeping out in the open and swimming whenever they want, because, as Joe says, "Swimming's no good. I don't seem to care for it, somehow, when there ain't anybody to say I shan't go in" (p. 138). But perhaps the most famous instance of this principle is the whitewashing episode, which casts Tom in the role of discovering it as a great law of human nature. The success of Tom's strategy rests on his intuitive discovery that people want to do what they are forbidden to. In order to change whitewashing from hard labor into the one thing the boys are mad to do Tom has only to present it as something he cannot allow them to do, an art requiring special skill which only he possesses, a task which he is under strict orders to perform only himself without help from anyone else. By means of this tactic Tom not only gets the boys to do the whitewashing for him; he gets them to pay him for the privilege.

The Adventures of Tom Sawyer is steeped in the rhythm of this relationship between adults and children. The delight of midnight trips is in creeping out of the window in answer to a secret signal and in defiance of an adult stricture. The pleasure of Huck Finn's society, like the attractiveness of his state, lies in its being forbidden. When Huck first enters the book, it is this angle from which he is viewed. Thus he is described as a "romantic outcast," a phrase which defines the point of view on him as Tom's. There is at this point no hint of what Huck's life might be like either from his point of view or the narrator's. The strong implication, however, is that the joys of his existence are imaginary, a product of prohibition. Huck is introduced in the book in great part as an element in Mark Twain's creation of the dynamic between pleasure and prohibition in the mind of Tom Sawyer. And Mark Twain's achievement in creating this dynamic in *The Adventures of Tom Sawyer* prepares us for Tom's passion for creating obstacles at the end of *Huckleberry Finn*. It is part and parcel of his conception of pleasure. If the adults have failed to fulfill their part of the game and provide difficulties for Tom to overcome, then he will simply have to play both parts and create the obstacles himself. That a new mode of pleasure has been discovered to the reader in the process of Huck's adventures is not Tom's fault; he is doing only what he thinks is expected of him.

Tom entertains his world and in return it provides the structures which make his pleasure possible and heaps on him all the attention he could possibly desire. The relationship between Tom and his community is remarkably positive and indeed it is so throughout the book. There are, however, aspects to this relationship which are a little darker than those so far discussed and which bring us to a further understanding of Tom's character, an understanding which begins to explain what happens to Tom in *Adventures of Huckleberry Finn*.

Tom's actions in the first half of *Tom Sawyer* are a series of entertainments, but they are also a series of exposures which reveal the absurdity and hypocrisy of his world. One of the basic hypocrisies which Tom exposes early in the book is that which lies behind the phrase "virtue rewarded." By "virtue" the community means hard, dull, stupid work and by "reward" it means a sense of pleasure and achievement in doing this hard, dull, stupid work. The exposure begins when Tom, having completed his whitewashing assignment, presents himself to Aunt Polly and reports that he is done. When she has assured herself that he is not lying, she proceeds to reward him with a choice apple and a "lecture upon the added value and flavor a treat took to itself when it came without sin through virtuous effort" (p. 21). The scene which precedes Aunt Polly's lecture has, of course, made a shambles of her premise. People do not enjoy what they work for; they enjoy what they play at. The "added value and flavor" of a treat come not through "virtuous effort" but through being told you cannot have it. But Aunt Polly herself no more acts on the basis of her scripture than Tom, for what she is now calling "virtuous effort" was just a few pages before hard work and punishment, something she would have to force Tom to do. The explosion of Aunt Polly's myth of human behavior, however, is built right into this scene: "And while she closed with a happy Scriptural flourish, he 'hooked' a doughnut" (p. 21).

The exposure of the hypocrisy of "virtue rewarded" continues in the scene in Sunday school in chapter 4. A certain kind of virtue is indeed rewarded in this incident but not exactly the kind the authorities pretend they wish to recognize. Outside the church on Sunday morning, Tom trades all the wealth he has gotten from selling whitewashing privileges the previous afternoon for Bible tickets. The exchange is certainly justified in Tom's eyes, for the opportunity to be called up in front of the entire Sunday school world to receive a Bible fulfills his ever-present dream of being the center of attention. But the tactic by which Tom wins his way to the Bible marks the absurdity of the terms of Judge Thatcher's presentation and expresses the absurdity of the "virtue rewarded" premise behind it:

> "That's it! That's a good boy. Fine boy. Fine, manly little fellow. Two thousand verses is a great many—very, very great many. And you never can be sorry for the trouble you took to learn them; for knowledge is worth more than anything there is in the world; it's what makes great men and good men; you'll be a great man and a good man yourself, someday, Thomas. . . . And you wouldn't take any money for those two thousand verses—no indeed you wouldn't" (pp. 40-41).

But Tom's exposure is made possible by the hypocrisy built into the situation and reflected in Judge Thatcher's speech. If the knowledge was its own reward, a thing which one would not take any money for, there would be no need for the bait of tickets yellow, red, and blue, and the Bible whose purchase they add up to. The very existence of these tickets defines the fact that no one would learn those verses without at least the dim possibility of having a moment of glory for it. All Tom does is to carry the implications of St. Petersburg Christianity to their logical conclusion, and thus there is a certain justice in his particular virtue being rewarded.

Tom's most dramatic exposure, however, occurs when he stages his own funeral and resurrection, for the situation he creates invites the adults to indulge in the hypocrisy of remorse:

"But it's *so* hard—oh, it's so hard! Only last Saturday my Joe busted a firecracker right under my nose and I knocked him sprawling. Little did I know then how soon—Oh, if it was to do over again I'd hug him and bless him for it."

"Yes, yes, yes, I know just how you feel, Mrs. Harper, I know just exactly how you feel. No longer than yesterday noon, my Tom took and filled the cat full of Pain-killer, and I did think the cretur would tear the house down. And God forgive me, I cracked Tom's head with my thimble, poor boy, poor dead boy" (pp. 131-32).

The situations which Aunt Polly and Mrs. Harper remember are such as to make clear the nature of their remorse. The absurdity of claiming you would hug a boy who has just set off a firecracker under your nose is patent. It could only happen if one had knowledge at the time of something that was to happen later. As this is impossible, so the formulations are absurd and unreal, a fact made quite clear when the boys return and thimble crackings and cuffings continue. The remorse is an emotional indulgence which ultimately has the effect of making the mourners feel good about themselves, because it implies that their actions are no real index of their hearts.

Tom's appearance at his own funeral exposes the hypocrisy at the heart of the adult's lament. His entrance is perfectly timed to accomplish this exposure with maximum effect. At just the moment when the minister has moved the entire congregation to tears and is himself openly weeping over the angelic picture he has created of the boys, Tom appears in all his bedraggled and mischievous reality. The illusion that the minister has created and the congregation conspired in is exploded and the unreality at the heart of the funeral exposed. As James Cox has noted, "Tom's joke, his play funeral, provides the ultimate definition of what the 'sincere' funeral was to have been for the town in the first place—an entertainment! A tearful, lugubrious, and hackneyed production in which each of the participants was fully working up his part—but an entertainment nonetheless."[2]

The adults are sufficiently happy to get the boys back that they do not mind being exposed as ridiculous. The potential humiliation of the scene is averted by the singing of "Old Hundred" and the final note is one of reconciliation and joy. But it has been a tight situation for a moment. Tom's series of exposures has culminated in something particularly egregious, for it is far harder to be exposed as an emotional hypocrite than a moral one. What is it that allows Tom to get away with this exposure? The answer lies in the discovery of a further dimension to the symbiotic relationship between Tom and the adults of St. Petersburg.

A number of critics who have written on *The Adventures of Tom Sawyer* have discussed the book in terms of its relation to the convention of Bad Boy literature which appeared in the United States, particu-

larly after the Civil War.[3] Books built around the character of the Bad
Boy sprang up as a reaction against an inundation of highly moralistic
juvenile fiction. This fiction pictured and exalted an unreal creature
who was totally good and spent all his time in memorizing the Bible
and going to church and taking care of his mother, and who reaped the
rewards of this earth and then those of heaven. It also pictured an evil
child who stole apples, lied to his mother, played hooky, and was
eventually hanged. It was against the background of this absurdity that
the Bad Boy books arose. Their hero, while called a Bad Boy to make
clear that he is not the Good Boy of the moralistic fiction, is in fact just
a real human boy, whose pranks, jokes, and rascalities are the natural
result of his energy and healthiness. The Bad Boy is not really bad, only
"mischievous," and it is clear that when he grows up he will be a pillar
of the community. The implication behind this literature is clear: socially useful adults develop only from real boys who have shown some
life as children. The rascality of such children is not negative; rather it is
understood and affirmed as a stage they must go through on their way
to becoming useful adults; it is indeed the indication that they will, in
fact, become useful adults.

The Adventures of Tom Sawyer is a paradigm of the Bad Boy convention, and its structure and hero can be most clearly understood in its
terms. There has been considerable critical debate on the structure of
Tom Sawyer since Walter Blair published, in 1939, his article, "On the
Structure of Tom Sawyer."[4] His thesis, most recently supported by
Hamlin Hill, Robert Reagan, and Albert Stone,[5] claims that the book
enacts Tom's growth from callow, unworthy childhood to worthy
maturity. Blair defined four major narrative strands in the story: "the
story of Tom and Becky, the story of Tom and Muff Potter, the Jackson's Island episode, and the series of happenings (which might be
called the Injun Joe story) leading to the discovery of the treasure."[6]
Each of these strands, according to Blair, "is initiated by a characteristic and typically boyish action. The love story begins with Tom's child-
ishly fickle desertion of his fiancée, Amy Lawrence; the Potter narrative
with the superstitious trip to the graveyard; the Jackson's Island episode with the adolescent revolt of the boy against Aunt Polly, and
Tom's youthful ambition to be a pirate; the Injun Joe story with the
juvenile search for buried treasure."[7]

Three of these strands, however, "are climaxed by a characteristic
and mature sort of action, a sort of action, moreover, directly opposed
to the initial action. Tom chivalrously takes Becky's punishment and
faithfully helps her in the cave; he defies boyish superstition and coura-
geously testifies for Muff Potter; he forgets a childish antipathy and
shows mature concern for his aunt's uneasiness about him."[8] The Injun
Joe story for Blair was "the least useful of the four so far as showing
Tom's maturing is concerned."[9] But surely there is no need for this

reservation, for in Blair's terms Tom's pity on discovering Injun Joe's death is a mature act, replacing his self-centered and seemingly callous earlier response. But, of course, the problem with Blair's analysis is precisely in the terms, for while he has accurately described a pattern in the book he has, I feel, inaccurately evaluated its meaning. Blair assumes certain actions to be "mature" and positive and other actions to be "immature" and negative without ever establishing the grounds for his classification and valuation. The closest he comes is to say that Tom's actions are mature because each of them "eventuates in an expression of adult approval."[10] In fact, the basis of Blair's thesis, and of the essays of those who support him, lies in the claim that Tom's progress in the book is a movement from bad to good and that this movement is defined as such by the changing reaction of the adult community to him. But clearly the adults in *Tom Sawyer* are in all essentials like the children: "Mr. Walters fell to 'showing off'. . . . The librarian 'showed off'. . . . and the little boys 'showed off'. . . . And above it all the great man sat and beamed a majestic judicial smile upon all the house, and warmed himself in the sun of his own grandeur—for he was 'showing off,' too" (p. 38). Indeed, the very "search for buried treasure," which Blair labels as "juvenile," is, upon Tom's success, taken up by every adult in St. Petersburg. If, in fact, the adults are in any way different from the children, the difference does not make them more positive than the children but more negative. The children admit, after all, that they are showing off to gain attention but the adults have to pretend that they are doing something else. The children are honest; the adults are hypocrites, a point which Tom's actions make again and again. Thus it hardly makes sense to assume that they provide the yardstick which charts a growth from something negative to something positive. In fact, it hardly seems accurate to describe Tom's change in the book as one of growth in this sense at all. One has only to compare the tone of the end of the book with that of the beginning to feel this. Indeed, in commenting on this ending, Blair does an about-face and finds that Tom's "adult" behavior in talking to Huck Finn means that he has "gone over to the side of the enemy."[11]

What Blair is responding to at the end of his article is Mark Twain's vision of the meaning of Bad Boy fiction as dramatized in *The Adventures of Tom Sawyer*. The structure of *Tom Sawyer* is at once an embodiment and an exposure of this convention and it takes its shape from the dynamics of the interaction between child and adult which lie behind the convention. Since the Bad Boy is just a natural child marked for the future as a solid, respectable citizen, he is the agent through whom the community can gain a temporary release which is dramatized in the conventional scene in which the Bad Boy licks the overly pious, unnatural Good Boy. But the Bad Boy does not hold any values which are at root different from those of the community, nor does he really intend to expose the hypocrisy of the values which the community holds and which the Good Boy is simply exaggerating. The Bad Boy is a rebel in that he temporarily flaunts and outrages the community, but he is a sanctioned rebel, because his rebellion is limited in time and intention; his rebellion is a stage which has respectability at its other end. The community wants, in fact demands, this rebellion, because it provides excitement and release, and because the ultimate assimilation of the rebellion constitutes a powerful affirmation of their values. The convention of the Bad Boy and the books that express it represent the form of rebellion without the reality, titillation without threat. They channel rebellion by confining it to a stage and sanctioning that stage, and ultimately they transform rebellion into affirmation.

The structure of *Tom Sawyer* is a perfect embodiment of this pattern. In the early part of the book Tom is consistently outrageous. He lies and steals and plays hooky as a matter of course. He hobnobs with Huck Finn against the express prohibition of the adults. He sneaks out at midnight to join the outcast in his adventure to the graveyard. There he watches a murder and makes no move to reveal the murderer. His early actions constitute a series of exposures, which culminates in his appearance at his own funeral. This is the height of Tom's rebellion and outrageousness, for in threatening to make the congregation look ridiculous in front of each other, in threatening to humiliate them, he pushes against the limits of what is sanctioned. Dignity is salvaged by the singing of "Old Hundred" but Tom's rebellion has reached its peak and from this point on his pattern of action changes.

In the first major scene after the resurrection episode, Tom is discovered in the ultimately approvable role, one which embodies to the highest possible degree the values of the community: he saves Becky not simply from the public humiliation of a whipping but from having to admit to herself or anyone else an interest in sex. He is here cast in the role of the true Southern gentleman. Such action clearly neutralizes the threat posed by his funeral and makes clear which side he is on. From this point on Tom adopts conventional values more and more explicitly. He becomes society's detective and exposes its murderer; indirectly he brings the murderer to bay and ultimately he kills him. He gets money and makes clear that he intends to invest it and make capital. In an extension of his role toward Becky, he saves her life and thus further adopts the conventional masculine role of protector of womanhood. In the final scene of the book, Tom, who began by longing for Huck's outcast state and by cordially hating along with him the confinements of clothes and schools, becomes the advocate of civilization, the adult who seeks to channel and transform the rebellion which threatens the community. As Henry Nash Smith has observed, "Mark Twain has written the Sunday-school story about the Good Little Boy Who Succeeded all over again with only a slight change in the hero's make-up and costume."[12] Thus Smith succinctly defines the essential similarity of the Bad Boy convention to the Good Boy literature which it was presumably attacking. And thus he succinctly defines the nature of Tom Sawyer's character and rebellion and the source of Mark Twain's final attitude toward Tom.

In spite of the negative undercurrents of the action and structure of *The Adventures of Tom Sawyer,* negative in terms both of Tom's relation to his community and of the narrator's and reader's attitude toward Tom, the tone of the novel is essentially genial and the character of Tom Sawyer emerges as essentially positive. Thus Robert Reagan is moved to call *Tom Sawyer* "the most amiable of all Mark Twain's novels,"[13] and Kenneth Lynn remarks, "Of all Twain's major fictions, *Tom Sawyer* is the only one in which an initiation ends neither in flight nor in catastrophe, but in serene and joyous acceptance."[14] For indeed the focus of *The Adventures of Tom Sawyer* is on the harmony between Tom and his community and on the satisfactions of the symbiotic relationship between them. Further, all Tom's characteristics are ultimately placed within this context and are made positive by it. Thus Tom's egotism, his overriding passion to be the center of attention, and his insistence on masterminding every action constitute the mode by which he both provides pleasure for the community and becomes useful to them. It is his egotism, his desire to be the center of attention, which leads him to create the situations which entertain and release them; it is equally these characteristics which in great part move him to testify for Muff Potter at the trial and to take Becky's whipping.

Of course, there are negative overtones to his character. His self-pity with its undercurrent of revenge and aggression, issuing in the desire to make people suffer for what they have done to him; his capacity to subordinate his sense to others' feelings to his desire for an effect; his insistence on things being done according to the rules—a characteristic which links him to the hypocrisy and rigidity which he is otherwise engaged in exploding and looks forward to what he will become in *Huckleberry Finn;* his genius in manipulating people—all of these qualities are present in Tom in *The Adventures of Tom Sawyer.* But they are either secondary and muted or they are transformed by the way they operate in the particular situation of this book. For, again, the focus of *The Adventures of Tom Sawyer* is on the pleasures of the relationship between Tom and his community, which is in essence the relationship between the entertainer and his audience. And in this study of the entertainer, his genius is the joy of his audience, and the necessary egotism, selfishness, and aggressiveness of his character are exculpated by this fact.

It is only at the very end of the book that the tone toward Tom becomes noticeably negative and we feel the presence of some new attitude, some new perspective. What we feel, of course, is the birth of *Adventures of Huckleberry Finn,* for the change in attitude toward Tom is intimately connected with the discovery of Huck Finn. It is only very late in *Tom Sawyer,* when Huck is separated from Tom by the necessities of the plot, that the possibilities of his character are discovered. It is only then that Huck is discovered as a voice, and a mask, and a point of view, one which will define Tom Sawyer differently and crystallize the perceptions about him which dominate the end of the book. What is wrong with the ending of *The Adventures of Tom Sawyer* is that it is the beginning of *Adventures of Huckleberry Finn* and *Huckleberry Finn* is a quite different book and in it Tom Sawyer is a quite different character.

From *Studies in the Novel,* 3 (Fall 1971), 293-304.

1. Samuel L. Clemens, *The Adventures of Tom Sawyer* in *The Writings of Mark Twain,* Definitive Edition (New York: Gabriel Wells, 1922-25), VIII, I. Subsequent references will be to this edition of *Tom Sawyer* and will be included in parentheses in the text.

2. *Mark Twain: The Fate of Humor* (Princeton: Princeton Univ. Press, 1966), p. 140.

3. The following are most important: Walter Blair, "On the Structure of *Tom Sawyer," MP,* 37 (1939), 75-88; John Hinz, "Huck and Pluck: 'Bad' Boys in American Fiction." *SAQ,* 51 (1952), 120-29; Jim Hunter, "Mark Twain and the Boy-Book in 19th-Century America," *CE,* 24 (1963), 430-38; Albert E. Stone, *The Innocent Eye: Childhood in Mark Twain's Imagination* (New Haven: Yale Univ. Press, 1961), pp. 58-90.

4. *MP,* 37 (1939), 75-88.

5. Hamlin Hill, "The Composition and the Structure of *Tom Sawyer," AL,* 32 (1961), 379-92; Robert Reagan, *Unpromising Heroes: Mark Twain and His Characters* (Berkeley: Univ. of California Press, 1966), pp. 117-21; Stone, pp. 78-89.

6. Blair, p. 84.

7. Ibid.

8. Ibid., pp. 84-85.

9. Ibid., p. 85.

10. Ibid.

11. Ibid., p. 88.

12. *Mark Twain: The Development of a Writer* (Cambridge, Mass: Harvard Univ. Press, 1962), p. 89.

13. Reagan, p. 116.

14. *Mark Twain and Southwestern Humor* (Boston: Little, Brown, 1959), p. 196.

ALLEN GUTTMANN

Mark Twain's *Connecticut Yankee:*
Affirmation of the Vernacular Tradition?

MOST CRITICS of Mark Twain's *Connecticut Yankee* have seen the
novel as a fierce attack upon Arthurian England and as a thorough-
going affirmation of nineteenth-century America (and of New England's technological triumphs); Gladys Bellamy has cautioned against
this overly simple reading:

> Instead of the popular interpretation as solely a celebration of
> American progress, the book may conceivably be viewed as a fic-
> tional working-out of the idea that a too-quick civilization breeds
> disaster. In brief, civilization must be organic.[1]

There are strong reasons for thinking that Mark Twain was indeed
skeptical of precipitant civilizing, that he had, in addition, serious
doubts about technology itself, that Hank Morgan, unlike the Mississippi river-pilots, is representative of something other than unmitigated
good. The *Connecticut Yankee* contains the same split, the same evidence of divided sensibility, that Van Wyck Brooks discovered in Mark
Twain himself; the genteel tradition and the vernacular tradition are at
war in the *Connecticut Yankee,*[2] and the Mark Twain who assaults
most vigorously the institutions of ancient Britain is *unable* to affirm
unambiguously the Hartford mechanic and his death-dealing machines.
Analysis of characterization and of action substantiate this assertion.

Many misreadings derive from an identification of Samuel Clemens
with The Boss. Twain himself pointed to the shortcomings of his hero:

> . . . this Yankee of mine has neither the refinement nor the weak-
> ness of a college education; he is a perfect ignoramus; he is boss of
> a machine shop; he can build a locomotive or a Colt's revolver, he
> can put up and run a telegraph line, but he's an ignoramus, never-
> theless.[3]

This external evidence is unnecessary, for Hank Morgan, at the very
onset, describes himself as practical and nearly barren of sentiment,
maker of guns, revolvers, cannon, boilers, engines. "Why, I could make
anything a body wanted—anything in the world, it didn't make any
difference what. . . ."[4] The Boss's code allows him to harness a pillar
hermit to a sewing-machine:

> I . . . got five years' good service out of him; in which time he
> turned out upward of eighteen thousand first-rate tow-linen
> shirts. . . . These shirts cost me nothing but just the mere trifle for
> the materials . . . and they sold like smoke to pilgrims at a dollar
> and a half apiece. . . . [5]

In not quoting this passage, Karl Marx missed an inordinate opportunity to frown at the heartless capitalist and the machinebound
worker. More striking and far less amusing is The Boss's determination
to rule England. Although he fights the brutal power of what the Angry
Young Men call "The Establishment," he himself is power-hungry and
continually boasting of the "couple of thousand men" under him.[6] His
early reaction is typical.

> I made up my mind to two things: if it was still the nineteenth
> century and I was among lunatics . . . I would presently boss that
> asylum or know the reason why; and if . . . it was really the sixth
> century . . . I would boss the whole country inside of three months.[7]

Hank Morgan professes his belief in American democracy and his dis-
gust with the inhumanity of Morgan le Fay & Co. is real, but he is
curiously eager to institute a standing-army and a West Point where his
"boys" can learn about "siege-guns, field-guns, Gatling guns, rifled
guns, smooth bores" and all the rest.[8] More than a similarity of names
links him to Morgan le Fay. The time comes when The Boss is indistin-
guishable from history's wittier despots, for he replaces feudal institutions with a "Bossism" complete with a censorship that involves sup-
pressing joke-books and hanging authors.[9] Eventually, The Boss admits
his "base hankering" to be president of an English republic, but long
before this admission he had espoused the theory of benevolent dictatorship. "Unlimited power is the ideal thing when it is in safe hands."[10]
Hank Morgan's impatience, ". . . there are times when one would like to
hang the whole human race and finish the farce," is but one omen of
ill.[11] Mark Twain shows us that Hank Morgan's hands are not safe; the
action demonstrates the horrible possibilities of technologically based
power. Dictatorship is all but attained as benevolence turns to violence.
— Analysis of the action leads to the same conclusion, for one can
scarcely miss noting that The Boss's wake is strewn with terror and with
corpses. His first "miracle," the eclipse, is revelatory. It consists chiefly
of blotting out the sun, of threatening a permanent substitution of
darkness for light.[12] This is, perhaps, a foreshadowing of the cataclysm
that ends the novel. Having thus miraculously won his freedom, The
Boss introduces technology by dynamiting Merlin's Tower.

> I made about three passes in the air, and then there was an awful
> crash and that old tower leaped into the sky in chunks, along with

a vast volcanic fountain of fire that turned night to noonday, and showed *a thousand acres of human beings groveling on the ground in a general collapse* of consternation.[13]

The dehumanized mob reappears at subsequent "miracles." In minor displays of prowess, the Yankee blows two offensive knights into "a steady drizzle of microscopic fragments" and shoots Sir Sagramor (plus nine other knights) in a remarkably allegorical conflict between the vernacular and the genteel forms of combat.[14] As the book draws to a close, the technological utopia becomes a holocaust. Besieged by a rebellious knighthood, The Boss, with the aid of Clarence, plans his defense carefully and efficiently—as a Yankee should. All that he had created he now destroys. "It was a pity, but it was necessary."[15] After exploding his dynamite torpedoes, The Boss comments, "Of course, we could not *count* the dead, because they did not exist as individuals, but merely as homogeneous protoplasm, with alloys of iron and buttons."[16] Electric fences and Gatling guns leave the fifty-four loyal "boys" and The Boss "masters of England."[17] Exulting, they examine the twenty-five thousand dead strewn comically about. The exultation ends when Merlin finally succeeds in getting his long-postponed revenge (by mesmerizing The Boss until the nineteenth century) and when the besieged realize that they have trapped themselves in their cave and must eventually succumb to "the poisonous air bred by those dead thousands."[18]

The experiment in "progress" is a failure. This failure is foreshadowed by metaphors. In a passage quoted above, Mark Twain uses the image of a "vast volcanic fountain of fire."[19] Later, Morgan le Fay is described as a "Vesuvius" who might at any moment "turn herself loose and bury a city."[20] The Boss's newspaper is entitled "*Camelot Weekly Hosannah and Literary Volcano*," a title which suggests both the praise lavished upon the semi-deified Boss and the impending catastrophe which his policies will bring.[21] And, as if circumventing the detractors of image-analysis, Mark Twain implies, in this same image, the final catastrophe; The Boss himself compares his clandestinely created nineteenth-century civilization to a "serene volcano, standing innocent with its smokeless summit in the blue sky and giving no sign of the rising hell in its bowels."[22] Nor is volcanic imagery the only clue reminding us that civilizations are dangerous play-toys. One need but consider the most dramatic scene in the novel, the "miracle" of the eclipse, to realize that The Boss's claims to complete control over nature are false. The great "miracle" of the eclipse is, in a sense, a lie, because Hank Morgan *cannot really* control the sun as he pretends to. The final catastrophic destruction of the technological civilization is but another way of proving that The Boss's pretensions were unfounded. The effort to control the forces of history fails disastrously when The Boss's own ingenious defenses create the trap which demonstrates his helplessness and the illusoriness of his power. Finally, in an almost prophetic passage, The Boss himself acknowledges the danger of Utopianism. When Sandy urges him to return a "bewitched" pigsty to its proper shape (a castle), The Boss demurs and replies that "in attempting a disenchantment without the true key, you are liable to err, and turn your hogs into dogs, and the dogs into cats, the cats into rats, and so on. . . ."[23] The Connecticut Yankee displays less caution in attempting to break the enchantment of the Arthurian Age, and he suffers the consequences. This is a remarkable parable for a civilization which, having turned Fort Dearborn into Chicago and the Russia of the Czars into the missile-launching empire of the Stalinists, shows frightening signs of ending, in the Boss's words, "by reducing . . . materials to nothing . . . or to an odorless gas. . . ."[24]

Thus considering The Boss's experiment with technological authoritarianism, it is difficult to agree that Mark Twain "glorifies the Yankee mechanic," or that he "was simply expressing the exuberance of his own character . . . in the person of that East Hartford Yankee. . . ."[25] Perhaps, but *this* Mark Twain is not the man who had Huck say, "Human beings *can* be awful cruel to one another." The Boss, although capable of insights like this, looks more and more like an enlarged version of Colonel Sherburn. I suspect that The Boss represents a turning-point in the hard road from ill-founded optimism to starkest nihilism. Mark Twain, when he finished the *Connecticut Yankee*, was a man who had lost his belief in the Idea of Progress. He had begun to fear that technology alone was not enough.

Thus characterization and action indicate that Mark Twain could attack Malory and the genteel tradition which Scott and Tennyson had projected backwards into the sixth century, but could *not* affirm whole-heartedly the vernacular tradition as embodied in The Boss and his Colt's Arms factory. He could reveal that the nobility of Camelot was as much a sham as that of the Grangerfords and Shepherdsons, but Huck, too weak to do more than cover Buck Grangerford's face and flee to the raft, is replaced by The Boss, made powerful by his technical knowledge, made ruthless by his power. The difference is the difference between the indecisive ending of *Huckleberry Finn* and the tragic chaos which is the logical conclusion to the *Connecticut Yankee*. As Santayana remarked, the humorist had nothing to offer in lieu of the rejected and satirized culture.

From *The New England Quarterly,* 33 (June 1960), 232-37.

1. *Mark Twain As A Literary Artist* (Norman, Oklahoma, 1950), 314.

2. These terms come, of course, from George Santayana's address, "The Genteel Tradition in American Philosophy," *Winds of Doctrine* (New York, 1912), and from John Kouwenhoven's *Made In America* (New York, 1948).

3. Quoted in Bellamy, *Mark Twain as Literary Artist,* 314.

4. Text used is that in *The Favorite Works of Mark Twain* (Garden City, New York, 1950), 657.

5. *The Favorite Works . . . ,* 759.

6. *The Favorite Works . . . ,* 657.

7. *The Favorite Works . . . ,* 664.

8. *The Favorite Works . . . ,* 776.

9. *The Favorite Works . . . ,* 858. This passage is amusing, but Southern jokes about Negroes are amusing too.

10. *The Favorite Works . . . ,* 859, 694.

11. *The Favorite Works . . . ,* 809.

12. *The Favorite Works . . . ,* 676-681.

13. *The Favorite Works . . . ,* 684. My italics.

14. *The Favorite Works . . . ,* 794, 856-857.

15. *The Favorite Works . . . ,* 877.

16. *The Favorite Works . . . ,* 877.

17. *The Favorite Works . . . ,* 883. This is, of course, an extraordinary emotion for the exemplar of American democracy.

18. *The Favorite Works . . . ,* 884.

19. *The Favorite Works . . . ,* 684.

20. *The Favorite Works . . . ,* 732-733.

21. *The Favorite Works . . . ,* 785.

22. *The Favorite Works . . . ,* 694. Mr. Leo Marx, to whom I am greatly in debt, both for method and for insights, tells me that imagery of the volcano is common among critics of nineteenth-century American democracy, e.g., J. F. Cooper's *The Crater.*

23. *The Favorite Works . . . ,* 742.

24. *The Favorite Works . . . ,* 742.

25. Van Wyck Brooks, *The Ordeal of Mark Twain* (New York, 1933), 282, 286.

F. R. LEAVIS

Mark Twain's Neglected Classic:
The Moral Astringency of *Pudd'nhead Wilson*

THE ATTITUDE of *Pudd'nhead Wilson* is remote from cynicism or pessimism. The book conveys neither contempt for human nature nor a rejection of civilization. It is concerned with the complexities of both human nature and civilization as represented in a historical community—for Dawson's Landing, it may reasonably be said, is one that, at a given time in actual American history, Mark Twain had intimately known.

We are not, by way of dismissing the suggestion of any general contempt, confined to adducing Wilson himself and the "fine, brave, majestic creatures" who uphold the code of the F.F.V. Most impressively, there is Roxy. It is true that her heroic maternal devotion plays against the extremity of mean heartless egotism given us in Tom. But her significance is not exhausted in that irony. We feel her dominating the book as a triumphant vindication of life. Without being in the least sentimentalized, or anything but dramatically right, she plainly bodies forth the qualities that Mark Twain, in his whole being, most values—qualities that, as Roxy bears witness, he profoundly believes in as observable in humanity, having known them in experience. Although born a slave, she is herself a "fine, brave, majestic creature," whose vitality expresses itself in pride, high-spiritedness, and masterful generosity. Her reckless presence at the duel defines Mark Twain's attitude towards the "code" more decisively than Wilson's participation does. When she proudly tells Tom that he is descended from the best blood of Virginia the effect, for all the irony, is not satiric. And her confident and justified reliance on the loyal comradeship, not only of her fellow-"niggers," but also of the officers of the *Grand Mogul,* has its part in the appraisal of human nature conveyed by the book as a whole.

Mr. De Voto makes the point that she represents a frank and unembarrassed recognition of the actuality of sex, with its place and power in human affairs, such as cannot be found elsewhere in Mark Twain. That seems to me true and important. It is an aspect of the general fact, that she is the presence in the book of a free and generous vitality, in which the warmly and physically human manifests itself also as intelligence and spiritual strength. It is this far-reaching associative way in which, so dominating a presence, she stands for—she *is*—triumphant life that gives the book, for all its astringency and for all the chilling irony of the close, its genial quality (to be both genial and astringent is its extraordinary distinction).

How far from satiric the spirit of *Pudd'nhead Wilson* is may be seen in the presentment of the subtleties of conscience and ethical sensibility in Roxy. Consider the episode of the stolen money and the threat to sell the Negro servants down the river. We are no doubt very close to the satiric note in the irony with which the chapter ends—in Percy Driscoll's self-gratulation on his magnanimity: "that night he set the incident down in his diary, so that his son might read it in after years and be thereby moved to deeds of gentleness and humanity himself." But we are remote from satire here:

> The truth was, all were guilty but Roxana; she suspected that the others were guilty, but she did not know them to be so. She was horrified to think how near she had come to being guilty herself; she had been saved in the nick of time by a revival in the colored Methodist Church, a fortnight before, at which time and place she had "got religion." The very next day after that gracious experience, while her change of style was fresh upon her and she was vain of her purified condition, her master left a couple of dollars lying unprotected on his desk, and she happened upon that temptation when she was polishing around with a dust-rag. She looked at the money awhile with a steadily rising resentment, and then she burst out with—"Dad blame dat revival, I wisht it had 'a be'n put off till to-morrow!"
>
> Then she covered the tempter with a book, and another member of the kitchen cabinet got it. She made this sacrifice as a matter of religious etiquette, as a thing necessary just now, but by no means to be wrested into a precedent; no, a week or two would limber up her piety, then she would be rational again, and the next two dollars that got left out in the cold would find a comforter—and she could name the comforter.
>
> Was she bad? Was she worse than the general run of her race? No. They had an unfair show in the battle of life. . . .

In spite of that last phrase, we know that what we have been contemplating is not just an exhibition of Negro traits: "her race" is the human race. These naive and subtle changes and adjustments of conscience and the moral sense we can parallel from our own inner experience. But there is nothing cynically reductive in Mark Twain's study of the moral nature of man; he shows the clairvoyance of a mind that is sane and poised, and the irony that attends the illustration of subtleties and complexities throws no doubt on the reality or the dignity or the effectiveness in human affairs of ethical sensibility.

I have not yet touched on the central irony of the book, the sustained and complex irony inherent in the plot. *Pudd'nhead Wilson* should be recognized as a classic of the use of popular modes—of the sensational and the melodramatic—for the purposes of significant art. The book, I have said, is not faultless, and an obvious criticism lies against the unfulfilled promise represented by the twins—the non-significant play made with them, their history and the sinister oriental dagger. Mark Twain, we can see, had intended to work out some interplay of the two parallel sets of complications: twins and interchanged babies. He abandoned the idea, but didn't trouble to eliminate that insistent focusing of expectation upon the twins. The fault is in a sense a large one, and yet it is not, after all, a very serious one: it doesn't affect the masterly handling of the possibilities actually developed.

The ironic subtleties that Mark Twain gets from the interchange of the babies in their cradles seem, as one ponders them, almost inexhaustible. There is the terrible difference, no more questioned by Roxy than by her master, between the "nigger" and the white. The conventionality of the distinction is figured by the actual whiteness of Roxy, whose one-sixteenth of Negro blood tells only in her speech (with which, indeed, it has no essential relation, as is illustrated later by the inability of "Valet de Chambers," now revealed as the pure-white heir, to shed the "nigger"-speech he learnt in childhood). So awful, ultimate and unchangeable is the distinction that Roxy, as, in order to save her child from the fate hanging over the slave (to be "sold down the river"), she changes the babies in their cradles, justifies herself by the example of God. The rendering is an irresistible manifestation of genius, utterly convincing, and done with a delicate subtlety of ironic significance:

> She flung herself on her bed and began to think and toss, toss and think. By-and-by she sat suddenly upright, for a comforting thought had flown through her worried mind:
> "Tain't no sin—*white* folks has done it! It ain't no sin, glory to goodness it aint't no sin! *Dey's* done it—yes, en dey was de biggest quality in de whole bilin', too—*kings!*"

She began to muse; she was trying to gather out of her memory the dim particulars of some tale she had heard some time or other. At last she said:

> "Now I's got it; now I 'member. It was dat ole nigger preacher dat tole it, de time he come over here fum Illinois en preached in de nigger church. He said dey ain't nobody kin save his own self—can't do it by faith, can't do it by works, can't do it no way at all. Free grace is de *on'y* way, en dat don't come fum nobody but jis' de Lord; en *he* kin give it to anybody he please, saint or sinner—*he*

don't kyer. He do jis' as he's a mineter. He s'lect out anybody dat
suit him, en put another one in his place, en make de fust one
happy for ever en leave t'other one to burn wid Satan."

There is of course a glance here at the Calvinism of Mark Twain's
youth. And it is to be noted that Roxy, while usurping the prerogative
of the predestinating Deity, has shown a wholly human compassion,
and has invoked a compassionate God in doing so:

> "I's sorry for you, honey; I's sorry, God knows I is—but what *kin* I
> do, what *could* I do? Yo' pappy would sell him to somebody,
> some time, en den he'd go down de river, sho', and I couldn't,
> couldn't, *couldn't* stan' it."

In saving the child from the consequences of the awful distinction that
she assumes to be in the nature of things, she demonstrates its lack of
any ground but convention; she demonstrates the wholly common
humanity of the "nigger" and the white. The father himself cannot
detect the fraud: he cannot tell his own child from the other. And—one
of the many ironies—it is his cruel, but confidently righteous, severity
that imposes the full abjectiveness of slave mentality upon his own
child, who becomes the defenseless and rightless servant of the slave's
child. On the other hand, Roxy's success in saving Valet de Chambers
(the name her proud tribute to an ideal "white" lordliness) from the
fate of the slave erects a dreadful barrier between child and mother.
Treated as "young Marse Tom," not only does he become that different
order of being, the "master"; in Roxy herself the slave attitudes that
she necessarily observes towards him find themselves before long at-
tended by the appropriate awe. When at last, outraged by the humiliat-
ing and cruel rebuffs that meet her appeal for a little kindness (she is in
need) to the old "nigger-mammy," she forgets habit and the ties of
motherhood, and pants for revenge, she has to recognize that she has
placed him in an impregnable position: no one will believe her tale. A
further irony is that, if he has turned out bad, a portent of egocentric
heartlessness, that is at least partly due to his spoiling as heir and young
master, the lordly superior being.

It is a mark of the poised humanity characterizing the treatment of
the themes of *Pudd'nhead Wilson* that, worthless and vicious as "Tom"
is, when he has to face the sudden revelation that he is a Negro, we feel
some compassion for him; we don't just applaud an irony of poetic
justice when he is cornered into reflecting, with an echo of his mother's
self-justifying recall of the Calvinistic God:

> "Why were niggers and whites made? What crime did the un-
> created first nigger commit that the curse of birth was decreed for

him? And why is this awful difference made between black and white?"

Compassion, of course, soon vanishes as the dialectic of utter selfishness unfolds in him. The developments of his incapacity for compassion are done with a convincingness that the creator of Tito Melema would have envied. When Roxy offers to be sold back into slavery in order to save "Tom" from being disinherited, and he, with dreadfully credible treachery, sells her "down the river," the opposite extremes of human nature are brought together in an effect that belongs wholly to the mode of *Pudd'nhead Wilson,* and is equally removed from melodrama and from cynicism. It can hardly be said, when we close the book, that the worst in human nature has not been confronted; yet the upshot of the whole is neither to judge mankind to be contemptible nor to condemn civilization. And it is remarkable how utterly free from animus that astringency is which takes on so intense a concentration in the close:

> Everybody granted that if "Tom" were white and free it would be unquestionably right to punish him—it would be no loss to anybody; but to shut up a valuable slave for life—that was quite another matter.
>
> As soon as the Governor understood the case, he pardoned Tom at once, and the creditors sold him down the river.

It is an irony of the tale that this, the fate to secure him against which Roxana had committed her crime, is, as an ultimate consequence of that crime, the fate he suffers.

From *Commentary,* 21 (February 1956), 133-36.

MARION MONTGOMERY

The New Romantic vs. the Old: Mark Twain's Dilemma in *Life on the Mississippi*

Romanticism is what we call the other fellow's idealism.

MARK TWAIN could refrain from social criticism in *Life on the Mississippi* no more than in his other works, but in this particular book the weakness of his position seems to be particularly underlined. Here clearly one has a case of the pot calling the kettle black, of one romantic chastising another for his romanticism. Sir Walter Scott, Louis XIV, and the Catholic Church are under constant attack, but in sharp contrast one sees Twain's personal and nostalgic romanticising of his life on the river two decades before the writing of the book, and, more exasperating, his mystical glorification of the industrial life of the late nineteenth century—the new romanticism so dear to Henry Grady.

The most genuine and charming portion of the book is that section which romanticizes his early life on the river. It is an endearing section because of its good-natured tolerance of rascals and its glorification of the heroes of river life. This aspect of Twain, the writer as historian, puts him closer to Sir Thomas Malory than he would wish to admit. The characters he lovingly remembers are frontier individualists—Captain Brown, the hard, proud pilot who abused his squire-cubs; the raftsmen who drank and swore and fought in the Mike Fink tradition which is really the Gawain tradition, the fights in both being more verbal than physical. One sees at the heart of these reminiscences a love of the river because it is proud and untamable and changeable and because it presents a constant challenge to heroism and ingenuity, a challenge whose reward is the exercise of heroism and ingenuity. There is expressed a love for those men who matched craftiness and stamina, sometimes foolishly, against the old dragon river or against a neighbor for the love of the match. The pilot, we are told in effect, is best when he is a Natty Bumppo without idealism: he needs the memory of a woodsman, and the cool judgment of a professional Indian fighter, but above all he ought to be a good liar.

But as Twain travels the river some twenty years after his own experiences, remembering the good old days and noticing the changes, he finds himself in a dilemma. He is torn between lamenting and praising the past and praising and preaching the future, caught in a middle age which is uncomfortable to him and confusing to the reader since he never faces up to the dilemma. He is joyful when he discovers one of the last of the rivermen, Captain Robert Styles of the *Gold Dust,* who keeps the tall tale alive even though he has to work at it superhumanly since the old dragon has been reduced to nothing but a river by new inventions and the U.S. Corps of Engineers. Still the Captain's tale of the engineers' struggle to keep the river dredged of alligators is almost as good as Gawain's slain dragons. And there is, happily, Uncle Mumford, the mate who still keeps alive the ancient ritual of "d——ing around when there is work to the fore." But the question that nags is whether the fine spotlight of the *Gold Dust,* which removes most of the perils that formerly challenged the pilot, is to be praised or condemned. And what of the new charts and buoys that make the job so safe and boring. Twain hears Uncle Mumford ridicule the efforts of government engineers to control the river, but he can't quite decide whether he believes they will or won't succeed. The truth seems to be that he hopes they won't for sentimental reasons but hopes they will in the interest of his abstract social ideal of the "genuine and wholesome civilization of the nineteenth century" represented by the factory and the locomotive. The dilemma is not an unusual one; it will likely be reflected in any person's thinking when he lives in a period of transition and is old enough to look backward with nostalgia but still young enough to look forward in youthful excitement. But Twain doesn't face up to the dilemma; he doesn't do so because he is intellectually committed to his second brand of romanticism, the mystical glorification of the industrial life to be, while emotionally committed to the first, the private memory of his youth.

If there is this hesitation in choosing between the good old days of the pilot and the present life of the pilot, there is none between the good old days of Europe's medieval life and that proud new dawn of American industrialism. Whenever Twain goes ashore below St. Louis, unless at Cairo, he is likely to end up in a free-for-all with Louis XIV, Sir Walter Scott, the Catholic Church, or all three. The hypocrisy of the Catholic Church in blessing the robbery of the Indians for the support of the monarchy is mercilessly pursued in the early chapters. But one detects in this criticism more hatred for the Church than sympathy for the Indians. Also Twain castigates knighthood for its haughtiness and snobbishness, then icily heaps ridicule upon the Arkansas peasants he sees along the shore. He can rail against the senseless jousts of *Ivanhoe* and see no paralled [sic] in the steamboat races in which not only the knight-pilot but the passengers as well are subjected to the dangers of exploding boilers through a pride the same in essence as that which led knights to the lists.

Twain is offended by the pretense of medievalism as exemplified by much of the architecture along the river in the South. Scott of course is responsible for the "sham castle" that is the capitol building of Baton

Rouge. "Admiration of his [Scott's] fantastic heroes and their grotesque 'chivalry' doings and romantic juvenilities still survive here in an atmosphere in which is already perceptible the wholesome and practical nineteenth century smell of cotton factories and locomotives." One whole chapter enlarges upon this theme by describing the typical planter's house. The description emphasizes the false and sentimental nature of the "House Beautiful" and its attachment to the past—the sham columns of pine, the *Godey's Lady's Books,* the inept drawings by the planter's daughters, the sentimental music stacked on the piano, the "inherited" bureau. But what Twain chooses to show as contrast to this pretentious planter's house is the pretentious pilot's steamboat which was rapidly becoming a relic of the past itself. We have described for us "chimney-tops cut to counterfeit a spraying crown of plumes—and maybe painted red; pilothouse, hurricane deck, boiler-deck guards, all garnished with white wooden filigree-work of fanciful patterns, . . . gilt deer-horns over the big bell; gaudy symbolic pictures on the paddlebox." What irritates one is that Twain describes the planter's house with sarcasm, the equally pretentious river boat with loving devotion faintly disguised by humor. He wants to be satirically realistic about others' romanticism but humorously sentimental about his own.

Whenever Twain turns attention away from life on the river to consider seriously the two social worlds of the late nineteenth century, the one located south of Cairo, the other north of St. Louis, the book suffers. For his sudden change from warm reminiscences to sometimes harsh social criticism often involves contradictory observations. For instance, he praises the New Orleans *Times-Democrat* issue of August 26, 1882 (the year industrial production caught up with agricultural), for its extended account of the year's business in the lower Mississippi valley. He praises the reporters as careful, responsible persons who know what they are about. "The editorial work is not back-grinding," he tells us seriously, "but literature." But shortly thereafter the same paper and the same writers are taken to task for using medieval prose derived from Scott's novels. Twain concludes that the only competent writer on the *Times-Democrat* is the editor. This criticism is wonderfully done through exaggeration, and one is led to believe from this instance that Twain comes closer to the truth when he is lying for humorous effect than when he tries to be serious.

Furthermore, whenever Twain goes north of St. Louis, he changes personality. The enlightened Candide just up from the South becomes a naive Dr. Pangloss in the land of the new dawn. "In Burlington, as in all these Upper-River towns, one breathes a go-ahead atmosphere which tastes good in the nostrils." The Utopia of the populous Northwest is praised in a manner worthy the president of a local chamber of commerce. They "fortify every weak place in their land with a school, a college, a library, and a newspaper; and they live under the law." One wonders what Eggleston would say to this evaluation of the area which he, as a resident, did not consider particularly forward in this same period. Twain catalogues the towns in his praise, but the praise is of their size. He can even praise Davenport for having two bishops resident, the Catholic and Episcopal, without getting red in the face, for such praise underlines the size. There is not even a hint that the Catholics of Davenport might be of the same superstitious nature as those of New Orleans or Rome.

Even though Twain professes a love of this new progress, the tour of Upper-River becomes progressively duller reading. He can't fool himself, even for the money he knew the book would bring him. There is some effort to praise the scenery, the sunset on the river, but in this "genuine and wholesome civilization of the nineteenth century" where the folks are full of "practical common sense, progressive ideas, and progressive works" Twain finds little that excites him to interesting comment. One is led to conclude it a good thing that he lived early enough to meet the rascals like the pilot Stephen who could cheat an innocent out of hard-earned money and then ridicule him into silence about repayment, could meet the liars like the old carpenter and professed killer in Hannibal, or the stubborn old fool, Captain Brown.

For Twain lived in the medieval period of American history at the court of the steamboat pilot, and that is the source of what is good in his work. Had he been born later he might have found the new utopia he believed appearing around him in the third quarter of the nineteenth century less congenial to his talents as appears evident from the work he did after the 1880's. But then, if one is to judge from the talent of some of the chamber of commerce testimonials quoted above, he might have done as well financially. He could have started as a cub in an advertising agency. And very likely he would have learned to joust with several hundred horses of sports car under him.

From *Mississippi Quarterly*, 11 (1958), 79-82.

ARTHUR L. SCOTT

The Innocents Abroad Revaluated

MARK TWAIN'S *The Innocents Abroad* (1869) is the most popular travel book ever written in America and yet has been the most unjustly abused by criticism. It has become a commonplace to think of Mark Twain as an ignorant, raucous frontiersman romping through venerable lands in 1867 with a sneer on his lips and a laugh in his throat—cultivating a contempt for everything foreign. A British reviewer found the book "offensive, . . . supremely contemptuous, . . . ostentatiously and atrociously vulgar," while the *New York Tribune* deplored its "offensive irreverence." In 1880 Henry Beers was complaining that the book gave us "a Europe vulgarized," and forty years later Gamaliel Bradford lamented, "It took me years to shake off the withering blight which Mark Twain's satire cast for me over the whole of Europe."

To be sure, *The Innocents Abroad* has found many to praise its humor and its honesty. But somehow, when critics discuss the tone of the book they seem almost always to fall back upon such phrases as "commercial philistinism" (Van Wyck Brooks), "shrieking Philistinism" (Archibald Henderson), "defiant Americanism" (Brooks, Carl Van Doren), and "roaring Americanism" (Edgar Lee Masters). The book is marred by obtrusive burlesque, we are told (C. Hartley Grattan, William B. Cairnes, F. O. Matthiessen); it displays a complete lack of historical imagination or feeling for the past (Beers, Mme. Blanc, Granville Hicks, Stuart P. Sherman); and it delights in irreverence towards everything which time and affection have honored (Blanc, Sherman, Bradford, Russell Blankenship, Arthur Hobson Quinn, Constance Rourke). Stuart Sherman summed up the prevailing attitude towards Twain as a traveler when he asserted:

> He is the kind of travelling companion that makes you wonder why you went abroad. He turns the Old World into a laughing-stock by shearing it of its storied humanity—simply because there is nothing in him to respond to the glory that was Greece, to the grandeur that was Rome—simply because nothing is holier to him than a joke. . . . he laughs at art, history, and antiquity from the point of view of one who is ignorant of them and mightily well satisfied with his ignorance.

Nor do our most recent and useful reference books attempt to dispel this traditional concept. Says *Literary History of the United States,* "The Innocents Abroad (1869) helped to belittle our romantic allegiance to Europe, feeding our emergent nationalism." And *The Oxford Companion to American Literature* describes the book merely as "a humorous narrative that . . . shows his [Twain's] typical American irreverence for the classic and the antique." Boorishness, philistinism, defiance, scorn, burlesque, irreverence, iconoclasm—these, plus humor, are the commonly mentioned ingredients of *The Innocents Abroad.* America's love for the volume is then partially explained by America's joy in discovering herself superior to the Old World on so many counts. In other words, the book supposedly helped destroy what V. F. Calverton calls our "colonial complex."

These conventional accusations contain a fund of truth, but are grossly misleading because they overlook important aspects of the book. Even Stuart Sherman later came to realize this, acknowledging that the rough iconoclastic Don Juan of *The Innocents Abroad* had "also a strain of Childe Harold." This strain of Childe Harold, strangely enough, has never been examined and is seldom even mentioned. Such an examination cannot help throwing a new and kindlier light upon the book, especially upon the European chapters, which have drawn far more adverse criticism than the later Holy Land chapters. (Incidentally, Hicks suggests that the more respectful mood of these late chapters is "pumped up piety for home consumption," and Brooks adds the insinuating comment, "besides, ancient Palestine was hardly a rival, as Europe was, of modern America." This seems like impugning motives where not feasible to condemn the performance.) Our brief study, therefore, will be restricted to the European section which has been most commonly misinterpreted.

From the start it was evident to his readers that Mark Twain was not a romantic traveler in the Irving-Longfellow tradition. Instead of padding his account with poetry and legends, he reveled in the trivialities of the foreign scene, frank to admit that his main interest was in novelties, whether they were ancient ruins or bearded ladies. On the one hand, he decided that French railroads were torture chambers on wheels, and that the soapless, rugless, lampless hotel rooms of Paris were little better. Well remembered, also, are his attempts to play billiards on the grotesque tables of the continent, and his excruciating experiences with the barbers of France and Italy. On the other hand, Twain had only praise for the public works of Napoleon III and for the magnificent turnpikes of Europe. In a frank confession of philistinism he said, "These things win me more than Italy's hundred galleries of priceless art treasures, because I can understand the one and am not competent to appreciate the other."

In spite of turnpikes and great public buildings, however, Mark

Twain found 1867 Europe woefully backward in material progress and did not hesitate to say so. He stressed the contemporary scene to an extent that has been criticized as a calculated sales device—a deliberate flattering of America's industrial civilization (Brooks, Blankenship, Quinn, Masters, Hicks, Rourke, Van Doren, Percy Boynton, Matthew Josephson, Stephen Leacock, Lewis Mumford). The truth is, however, that, although he considered life much more arduous and primitive in Europe than in America, Mark Twain made significant comparison between material conditions at home and abroad on only one occasion— the well-known description of an imaginary Italian's travels in the United States.

Like thousands of other travelers, Twain was merely discovering with naive surprise that Europe was behind America in manufactured luxuries. It does not follow, however, that this surprise implies any criticism of Europe's treasures or even has any connection with satire on those things which the Old World holds most sacred. And yet the notion persists that Twain reduced everything in Europe to the level of a Yankee drummer, setting a slur of commonness upon beauty and splendor. According to Russell Blankenship, the book's motto is, "If you don't understand it, laugh at it." And Arthur Hobson Quinn calls the book valueless because of the "*nil admirari*" attitude of the author.

Let us take a few examples. Detractors point to Twain's description of the Cathedral of Notre Dame as a "brown old Gothic pile ... clustered thick with stony, mutilated saints"; but they neglect to mention that these few lines are followed by a page of romantic musings about the sights which these saints have witnessed down through the ages. Frequently called to attention also is Twain's disappointment in the "coarse mosaics" and "unlovely Byzantine architecture" of St. Mark's in Venice; but no one reminds us that he swiftly added that the cathedral's "hoary traditions make it an object of absorbing interest to even the most careless stranger." And again we are told that to him the Church of St. Peter in Rome "did not look nearly so large as the capitol, and certainly not a twentieth part as beautiful, from the outside"; but we are not informed that these two lines are followed by four pages of awed description of St. Peter's and the view from its dome, or that Twain finally confessed, "Its height and size would represent two of the Washington capitol set one on top of the other—if the capitol were wider."

Twain's refusal to accept the conventional estimate of medieval architecture does not prove that he was irreverently grinning at the august beauties of Europe. Actually, it made him uncomfortable to give an honest, disillusioned report, such as he gave about the dilapidated buildings and garbage-laden canals of Venice: "It seems a sort of sacrilege to disturb the glamour of old romance that pictures her to us softly from afar off as through a tinted mist, and curtains her ruin and her desolation from our view." He is more relaxed and more eloquent, as a matter of fact, when he is praising Europe than when he is finding fault. Note for instance his rhapsody on Versailles:

> Versailles! It is wonderfully beautiful! You gaze, and stare, and try to understand that it is real, that it is on the earth, that it is not the Garden of Eden—but your brain grows giddy, stupefied by the world of beauty around you, and you half believe you are the dupe of an exquisite dream. The scene thrills one like military music! . . . It was worth a pilgrimage to see.

Four pages of enraptured description follow this opening and they certainly are not the words of "a travelling companion that makes you wonder why you went abroad." Nor was Mark Twain completely unresponsive even to architectural splendors. No fair-minded critic should overlook the chapter devoted almost entirely to chanting the marvels of Milan Cathedral, calling it "a vision!—a miracle!—an anthem sung in stone, a poem wrought in marble!" These pages are alive with wonderment and replete with superlatives such as, "Surely, it must be the princeliest creation that ever brain of man conceived."

Palpably unjust, moreover, is the charge that Mark Twain was deficient in historical imagination and sympathy, was arrogantly candid, and determined not to sink his identity into the object contemplated. It almost seems that there is a conspiracy among critics not to mention Twain's sober contemplations on the Bridge of Sighs, his musings in the dungeons of Edmund Dantes and the "Iron Mask," his awed respect for the Coliseum, his marveling over "the royalty of heart and brain" buried in the great cemetery of Père la Chaise in Paris, his meditations before the Duomo in Pisa, his emotionalism over an ancient tear-jug, his romantic dreams atop the renowned Acropolis in Athens and elsewhere. Nor is it fair to laugh off as farce Twain's imaginative recreation of the past amid the ruins of Pompeii. Whatever his faults may be, a want of historical imagination is certainly not among them.

> Day after day and night after night we have wandered among the crumbling wonders of Rome; day after day and night after night we have fed upon the dust and decay of five-and-twenty centuries— have brooded over them by day and dreamt of them by night till sometimes we seem mouldering away ourselves, and growing defaced and cornerless.

Indeed, a sense of the past—colorful and exciting—enriches chapter after chapter of *The Innocents Abroad*. In Venice Twain wrote, "A part of our being has remained still in the nineteenth century, while another part of it has seemed in some unaccountable way walking among the phantoms of the tenth." And the glory that was Greece moved him in the same manner.

> What cared we for outward visions when Agamemnon, Achilles, and a thousand other heroes of the great Past were marching in ghostly procession through our fancies? What were sunsets to us, who were about to live and breathe and walk in actual Athens, yea, and go far down into the dead centuries and bid in person for the slaves, Diogenes and Plato, in the public market-place. . . .

Can this be the ignorant buffoon who, we are told, laughs at antiquity because nothing is holier to him than a joke? It is possible that passages of this nature—even though numerous—are often shrugged off as not reflecting the "real" Mark Twain, who is known to be a humorist and who is allegedly scornful of everything foreign and of everything old.

The touchstone of Twain's so-called *nil admirari* attitude seems to be his supposed hatred of medieval art. Even here the critics fail to understand his attitude. As a democrat, of course, he loathed the patronage system which caused the "old masters" to prostitute their noble talents "to the adulation of such monsters as the French, Venetian, and Florentine Princes," but this was not the real trouble. In a word, the real trouble was merely surfeit. "I like to look at pictures," he wrote; but the weary miles of faded, gloomy paintings dulled his sensibilities by their remorseless demand for admiration. Every tourist knows this feeling. When he saw a gorgeous painting hung in a room by itself, he was quick to acknowledge, ". . . possibly, what I have been taking for uniform ugliness in the galleries may be uniform beauty after all."

It should also be remembered that Mark Twain lampooned not the paintings themselves, but rather the humbugs who threw themselves into pretended raptures over them. Never "satisfied with his ignorance," he confessed envy of those people who truly understood and loved art. "If I did not so delight in the grand pictures that are spread before me every day of my life by the monarch of all old masters, Nature," he said, "I should come to believe, sometime, that I had in me no appreciation of the beautiful whatever."

Although no one has been so rash as to accuse Mark Twain of insensitivity to the glories of nature, even in Europe, yet almost no one mentions that *The Innocents Abroad* is distinguished for its vivid descriptions of the natural beauties of the Old World. The Bois de Boulogne, the countryside of France, Lake Como, Vesuvius, the Blue Grotto, Venice and Athens by moonlight—are not these glorious word-pictures as much a part of the book as are the dirt and vermin of Civita Vecchia? "Put Mark Twain on to mountain, lake, storm at sea, a prairie fire, or a volcano," H. R. Haweis of England once observed, "and you need not pull out your photographic apparatus."

Not only is Twain's love for picturesque nature ignored, but it is generally believed that his attitude towards the *objets d'art* (apart from the "old masters") of Europe was one of derisive ignorance. Readers remember how Twain and his friends baited their guides by feigning bland indifference to everything; but we should never forget that this was merely a pose: "We came very near expressing interest, sometimes, even admiration," he said, "It was very hard to keep from it." He had his favorite paintings like Raphael's "Transfiguration"; he was entranced by the snowy sculptures in a Genoese cemetery and by the bronzes, cameos, and delicate engravings of Pompeii. The cracked and century-stained statues of "Laocoön" and "The Dying Gladiator" captured his imagination as few pictures had done. Significant, also, are his musings upon the ancient tear-urn presented to him by a Pisan antiquary:

> It spoke to us in a language of its own; and with a pathos more tender than any words might bring, its mute eloquence swept down the long roll of the centuries with its tale of a vacant chair, a familiar footstep missed from the threshold, a pleasant voice gone from the chorus, a vanished form! . . . No shrewdly-worded history could have brought the myths and shadows of that old dreamy age before us clothed with human flesh and warmed with human sympathies so vividly as did this poor little unsentient vessel of pottery.

These are not the words of a man who lacks sympathy for the past and who therefore takes "malignant joy" in mocking all the holy objects in the temple of Europe. To be sure, Mark Twain is capable of mocking the past, as he shows in his well-known travesty on the gladiatorial bouts in the ancient Coliseum. This travesty, however, casts no aspersions on a cherished institution, because the bloody arena of Rome has hardly been honored by time. As for his extended satire on Pierre Abelard: this surely contains none of that "heavy smartiness" of which F. O. Matthiessen complains, for here Twain is savagely in earnest. To him, this so-called "romance of the twelfth century" is simply a coldblooded seduction of the innocent Heloise by a scoundrel who later refuses to share in her disgrace. In this case Twain robs history of its glamor not to make a joke, but to examine a sentimental tradition in the clear white light of reality. If we place these few unconventional pictures of the past over against his numerous dreamy meditations on olden times, we will have to confess that Mark Twain is surprisingly respectful of Europe's history and remarkably well informed about it.

His respect for the European past, however, did not extend to certain historical institutions which were still flourishing. In fact, his condemnation of the Italian Church and of several monarchies is often cited to illustrate his alleged contempt for foreign institutions. In both instances, however, his indictments were based upon high principles. For fifteen centuries, cried Twain, the Church in Italy had bled the people, turning all its wealth and energies to raising up a grand array of edifices—and starving half the citizens to do it. He confined his strictures solely to the temporal despotism of the Church. He denounced not religion, but rather an institution which seemed to have abandoned religion in its lust for wealth and power. The Italian Church, he felt, had forfeited its right to be revered. At the same time, he was quick to praise those Dominican friars who had risked their lives during the recent cholera epidemic. As an English clergyman observes regarding *The Innocents Abroad,* "The value of religion itself is not more tenderly, than is the sham and cant of hypocrisy severely handled."

Twain's diatribes against the Greek and Ottoman monarchies have precisely the same basis in humanitarianism. As yet he was far from his later belief that all thrones were nothing but "perpetuated piracy." For Napoleon III of France and for the Czar of Russia he expressed great admiration, because of their public works and reforms. But George I of Greece was a different matter. Him Twain excoriated as a "small tyrant" who indulged in a hundred personal extravagances while trying to ape the "great monarchies." National poverty was the inevitable result and the manly people of Greece were now reduced to "only a tribe of unconsidered slaves." As for the neighboring Sultan, Mark Twain flayed him as the genius of Ignorance, Bigotry, and Indolence—the titular head of a government whose three graces were Tyranny, Rapacity, and Blood. This was monarchy in its most degenerate form. Stupid and feeble as his meanest slave, said Twain, Abdul Aziz reclined dully among his eight hundred concubines, while his mother and the Premier plundered his wretched realm.

Mark Twain, then, distinguished between benevolent and malevolent despots by comparing their subjects. The welfare of the common man underlay his criticism of church and state, of industry and street life. Without favor, governments and smoking tobaccos were judged by their benefits to the ordinary individual. Actually, tobaccos were judged more often than governments, for it was the trivialities of the foreign scene which interested Mark Twain: barbers, billiard tables, hotel bedrooms, Turkish coffee, baths and *narghilis*, shopkeepers, guides, the *can-can*, beggars, mangy dogs, policemen, menus, and modes of travel. These were typical comic fodder for Twain in Europe, and it should be noted that none of these things is particularly reverend.

The fact is—and this we should not forget—that the humor and satire of *The Innocents Abroad* are seldom directed against cherished or important aspects of foreign life. Instead, they derive almost wholly from the minutiae of the scene and from the pilgrims themselves, the author included. It is time we recognized, especially, that Twain himself and his fellow innocents are the butt of as much fun as everything European combined. Many readers, indeed, find their chief enjoyment in the portraits of the Oracle, the Poet Lariat, Interrogation Point, the Old Traveller, the arrogant industrialist, the poor miserable hermaphrodite Frenchman. The pilgrims are satirized bitingly (although with more mercy than in the forty-nine *Alta* letters upon which the book is based) for their somberness, their self-pamperings, their penny-pinching, their boundless absurdities—and especially for their vandalism, which is in striking disharmony with their feigned ecstasies over the treasures of Europe.

And finally, the prevailing inference is mistaken that Mark Twain disliked the continental way of life in general. Critics recall too readily only his pictures of the sloth, backwardness, squalor, oppression, and shamelessness in Italy. These pictures are vivid, shocking. He was not immune, nevertheless, to that peculiar charm of life which was luring many an American exile to this same Italy. Barren as Europe was of physical luxuries, Mark Twain felt the attraction of continental living and later partook of it with his family for about ten years. In any fair analysis of *The Innocents Abroad*, passages like the following simply cannot be overlooked:

> Afterwards we walked up and down one of the most popular streets [of Milan] enjoying other people's comfort and wishing we could export some of it to our restless, driving, vitality-consuming marts at home. Just in this one matter lies the main charm of Europe—comfort. In America, we hurry—which is well; but when the day's work is done, we go on thinking of our losses and gains, we plan for the morrow, we even carry our business cares to bed with us, and toss and worry over them when we ought to be restoring our racked bodies and brains with sleep. We burn up our energies with these excitements, and either die early or drop into a lean and mean old age at a time of life which they call a man's prime in Europe. . . .
>
> I do envy these Europeans the comfort they take. When the work of the day is done, they forget it. Some of them go, with wife and children, to a beer hall, and sit quietly and genteelly drinking a mug or two of ale and listening to music; others assemble in the great ornamental squares in the early evening to enjoy the sight and the fragrance of flowers and to hear the military bands play—no European city being without its fine military music at eventide; and yet others of the populace sit in the open air in front of the refreshment houses and eat ices and drink mild beverages that could not harm a child. They go to bed moderately early, and sleep well. They are always appreciative of life and its manifold blessings. One never sees a drunken man among them. The change that has

come over our little party is surprising. Day by day we lose some of our restlessness and absorb some of the spirit of quietude and ease that is in the tranquil atmosphere about us and in the demeanor of the people. We grow wise apace. We begin to comprehend what life is for.

Sentiments of this nature have been ignored by those critics who believe with Van Wyck Brooks that *The Innocents Abroad* "buttressed the feeble confidence of our busy race in a commercial civilization." That Mark Twain loved money and luxuries is true. It is wrong, however, to infer from this that he consequently surveyed unprogressive Europe with a jaundiced eye.

In conclusion, one bit of historical information which helps give proper perspective to our view of *The Innocents Abroad.* To anyone familiar with Twain's early journalistic writings, the wonder is not that he found so much to ridicule in Europe, but that he found so much to praise. Reared in the rough frontier tradition of irreverence, farce, and satire, Mark Twain for several years prior to his *Quaker City* voyage had been blasting countless aspects of life from San Francisco to New York City. In other words, the satire and censure of his first travel book do not spring from any "defiant Americanism," but are directly in the vein of his early journalism. The barbs aimed at Europe in the book, as a matter of fact, are blunt indeed compared to some of the barbs scattered throughout his early sketches of America.

It cannot be denied that Mark Twain wrote of Europe from the viewpoint of an American Westerner who was ignorant of many cultural values. He did not, however, completely lack the humility of his ignorance, as most critics would have us believe. Already he thirsted for knowledge and culture. A frank modernist, he was often more interested in the emergence of the new than in the enduring of the old; but never did he shear antiquity of its storied humanity simply to make a joke. The iconoclasm of Don Juan was so well balanced by the romantic enthusiasm of Childe Harold that *The Innocents Abroad* was in little danger of becoming the vulgar, derisive, farcical, belligerently nationalistic volume that it is so frequently called. It is time that we ceased repeating the traditional nonsense that Mark Twain looked at Europe in the same way that his own Barclay Goodson looked at old Sawlsberry—"like as if he was hunting for a place that he could despise the most."

From *Western Humanities Review,* 7 (Summer 1953), 215-23.

SELECTED BIBLIOGRAPHY

Bibliography

Asselineau, Roger. *The Literary Reputation of Mark Twain From 1910 to 1950.* Paris: Librairie Marcel Didier, 1954; rpt. Westport, Conn.: Greenwood, 1971.

Branch, Edgar M. "A Chronological Bibliography of the Writings of Samuel Clemens to June 8, 1867." *American Literature,* 48 (May 1946), 109-59.

Brashear, Minnie M. "Mark Twain Juvenilia." *American Literature,* 2 (March 1930), 25-53.

Johnson, Merle. *A Bibliography of the Works of Mark Twain.* New York: Harper, 1910.

Leary, Lewis. *Articles on American Literature, 1900-1950.* Durham, N.C.: Duke Univ. Press, 1954; supplemented by *Articles on American Literature, 1950-1967,* 1970.

Literary History of the United States. Ed. Robert E. Spiller, et al. New York: Macmillan, 1948, III, 689-96; Bibliographical Supplement, ed. Richard M. Ludwig, New York: Macmillan, 1959, pp. 178-80.

Long, E. Hudson. *Mark Twain Handbook.* New York: Hendricks House, 1958.

Stovall, Floyd, et al. *Eight American Authors: A Review of Research and Criticism.* New York: Norton, 1963; rev. ed. by James Woodress, 1971.

Works

Mark Twain's Letters, Arranged with Comment ed. Albert Bigelow Paine. 2 vols. New York: Harper, 1917.

The Writings of Mark Twain, ed. Albert Bigelow Paine. 37 vols. New York: Gabriel Wells, 1922-25.

Mark Twain's Autobiography, ed. Albert Bigelow Paine. 2 vols. New York: Gabriel Wells, 1925. (Vols. 36-37 of *The Writings of Mark Twain*).

Mark Twain's Notebook, ed. Albert Bigelow Paine. New York: Harper, 1935.

Mark Twain in Eruption, ed. Bernard De Voto. New York: Harper, 1940. A third volume of the autobiography of Mark Twain.

The Autobiography of Mark Twain, ed. Charles Neider. New York: Harper, 1959. Reissued Harper & Row, 1966. A fourth volume of the autobiography of Mark Twain rearranging Paine's and De Voto's work and adding some passages.

N. B. The Iowa-California edition of Twain's works—to comprise twenty-four volumes—is currently appearing and will supersede the Paine edition.

The *Mark Twain Papers,* under the general editorship of Frederick Anderson of Berkeley, are currently appearing and will ultimately comprise approximately fifteen volumes.

Biography

Brashear, Minnie N. *Mark Twain: Son of Missouri.* Chapel Hill: Univ. of North Carolina Press, 1934.

Brooks, Van Wyck. *The Ordeal of Mark Twain.* New York: Dutton, 1920; rev. ed. 1933.

Clemens, Clara. *My Father, Mark Twain*. New York: Harper, 1931.

De Voto, Bernard. *Mark Twain's America*. Boston: Little, Brown, 1932.

Ferguson, DeLancey. *Mark Twain: Man and Legend*. New York: Bobbs-Merrill, 1943.

Henderson, Archibald. *Mark Twain*. London: Duckworth, 1911.

Howells, William D. *My Mark Twain: Reminiscences and Criticism*. New York: Harper, 1910.

Kaplan, Justin. *Mr. Clemens and Mark Twain*. New York: Simon & Schuster, 1966.

Paine, Albert Bigelow. *Mark Twain: A Biography*. 3 vols. New York: Harper, 1912.

Wagenknecht, Edward G. *Mark Twain: The Man and His Work*. New Haven: Yale Univ. Press, 1935; rev. ed. Norman: Univ. of Oklahoma Press, 1961, 1967.

Wecter, Dixon. *Sam Clemens of Hannibal*. Boston: Houghton Mifflin, 1952.

Criticism

I. *1870-1900:*

Bentzon, Therese. "Les Humoristes Americains: I. Mark Twain." *Revue des Deux-Mondes,* 100 (15 July 1875), 313-35.

Kipling, Rudyard. "An Interview with Mark Twain," in *From Sea to Sea.* 2 vols. New York: Doubleday and McClure, 1899.

Lang, Andrew. "Mr. Lang on the Art of Mark Twain." *The Critic,* 16 (25 July 1891), 45-46.

Matthews, Brander. "Mark Twain—His Work." *Book-Buyer,* 13 (January 1897), 977-79.

Thompson, C. M. "Mark Twain as an Interpreter of American Character." *Atlantic Monthly,* 79 (April 1897), 443-50.

Trent, W. P. "Mark Twain as an Historical Novelist." *The Bookman,* 3 (May 1896), 207-10.

Twichell, Joseph H. "Mark Twain." *Harper's Magazine,* 92 (1896), 817-27.

II. *1900-1925:*

Ade, George. "Mark Twain as Our Emissary." *The Century Magazine,* 81 (December 1910), 204-06.

Ellsworth, William W. *A Golden Age of Authors.* Boston: Houghton, Mifflin, 1919.

Howells, William D. "Mark Twain: An Inquiry." *North American Review,* 172 (February 1901), 306-21.

Matthews, Brander. "Mark Twain and the Art of Writing." *Harper's Magazine,* 141 (October 1920), 635-43.

Pattee, Fred L. *A History of American Literature Since 1870.* New York: Century, 1915.

Perry, Bliss. *The American Mind.* Boston: Houghton, Mifflin, 1912.

Perry, Bliss. *The American Spirit in Literature.* New Haven: Yale Univ. Press, 1918.

Sherman, Stuart P. "Mark Twain." *The Cambridge History of American Literature.* New York: Putnam, 1921, III, pp. 1-20.

III. *1925-1950:*

Blair, Walter. *Native American Humor.* New York: American Book, 1937.

Blankenship, Russell. *American Literature as an Expression of the National Mind.* New York: Henry Holt, 1931.

Cowie, Alexander. *The Rise of the American Novel.* New York: American Book, 1948.

Ferguson, DeLancey. "Huck Finn Aborning." *Colophon,* n.s., 3 (Spring 1938), 171-80.

Fiedler, Leslie. "Come Back to the Raft Ag'in, Huck Honey!" *Partisan Review,* 15 (June 1948), 664-71.

Hazard, Lucy L. *The Frontier in American Literature.* New York: Crowell, 1927.

Liljegren, Sven B. *The Revolt Against Romanticism in American Literature As Evidenced in the Works of Samuel L. Clemens.* Upsala: Publications of the American Institute of the Univ. of Upsala, 1947.

Masters, Edgar Lee. *Mark Twain: A Portrait.* New York: Scribner's, 1938.

Parrington, Vernon L. *The Beginning of Critical Realism in America, 1860-1900.* New York: Harcourt, Brace, 1930.

Quinn, Arthur H. *American Fiction: An Historical and Critical Survey.* New York: Appleton-Century, 1936.

Rourke, Constance. *American Humor: A Study of the National Character.* New York: Harcourt, Brace, 1931.

Trilling, Lionel. Introduction to *The Adventures of Huckleberry Finn.* New York: Rinehart, 1948.

Van Doren, Carl. *The American Novel, 1789-1939.* New York: Macmillan, 1940.

Wecter, Dixon. "Mark Twain." *Literary History of the United States.* New York: Macmillan, 1948.

IV. 1950-

Andrews, Kenneth R. *Nook Farm—Mark Twain's Hartford Circle.* Cambridge: Harvard Univ. Press, 1950.

Baldanza, Frank. *Mark Twain: An Introduction and Interpretation.* New York: Barnes & Noble, 1961.

Bellamy, Gladys C. *Mark Twain as a Literary Artist.* Norman: Univ. of Oklahoma Press, 1950.

Branch, Edgar M. *The Literary Apprenticeship of Mark Twain.* Urbana: Univ. of Illinois Press, 1950.

Canby, Henry S. *Turn West, Turn East—Mark Twain and Henry James.* Boston: Houghton Mifflin, 1951.

Covici, Pascal, Jr. *Mark Twain's Humor: The Image of a World.* Dallas: Southern Methodist Univ. Press, 1962.

Cox, James. *Mark Twain: The Fate of Humor.* Princeton: Princeton Univ. Press, 1966.

Eliot, T. S. Introduction to *The Adventures of Huckleberry Finn.* New York: Chanticleer, 1950.

Ensor, Allison. *Mark Twain & the Bible.* Lexington: Univ. of Kentucky Press, 1969.

Foner, Philip S. *Mark Twain: Social Critic.* New York: International Publishers, 1958.

Geismar, Maxwell. *Mark Twain: An American Prophet.* Boston: Houghton Mifflin, 1970.

Marx, Leo. "Mr. Eliot, Mr. Trilling, and *Huckleberry Finn.*" *The American Scholar,* 22 (Autumn 1953), 423-40.

Smith, Henry Nash. *Mark Twain: The Development of a Writer.* Cambridge: Belknap Press of Harvard Univ. Press, 1962.

Spiller, Robert E. *The Cycle of American Literature: An Essay in Historical Criticism.* New York: Macmillan, 1955; rpt. New York: New American Library, 1957.